D0810276

Ben Carpenter

THE BIGS

The Secrets _You_ Need to Know to Succeed in College and Beyond

- EXPLORING CAREERS
- FINDING INTERNSHIPS
- GETTING A GREAT JOB
- STARTING A BUSINESS
- BEING A LEADER
- LIVING A HAPPY LIFE

THE BIGS PROJECT

The Bigs Project
22 Round Hill Club Road
Greenwich, CT 06831
www.thebigsproject.com

Library of Congress Cataloging-in-Publication Data is available through the Library of Congress.

ISBN: 978-099660-710-0

Cover and interior design by Gary A. Rosenberg
www.thebookcouple.com

Printed in the United States of America

10   9   8   7   6   5   4   3   2   1

This book is dedicated to my wife Leigh—
who has made my hopes and dreams come true
for the past 30 years.

Contents

Chapter 1

Hopes and Dreams

Growing up, I never heard anyone talk about hopes and dreams. I had loving parents who sacrificed everything for their children, but life was a struggle and the focus was on getting through each day.

The first person I heard talk about dreams was Ted Knetzger—the founder of the company where I spent most of my career. Ted had a unique combination of practicality and generosity, and his heartfelt belief was that helping his employees realize *their* hopes and dreams would allow him to realize his own.

I was fortunate to have a role model from whom to learn the power of dreams and how to accomplish them. The purpose of *The Bigs* is to pass this knowledge on to you.

THE BIG LEAGUES

In baseball, "the bigs" is slang for the big leagues. When you become responsible for yourself, and you're being paid to do a job, you're in the big leagues. This applies not only to business, but to all industries, because *the same funda-mental principles that lead to successful and rewarding careers in teaching, technology, construction, or consulting also apply to public relations, healthcare, firefighting, or finance.*

This book is the story of my 35-year corporate and entrepreneurial career and the lessons I learned from my wide range of jobs—most notably as a bar owner and a Wall Street CEO. Since these stories and lessons come from my experiences, you need a little background to understand them.

IS THIS OKAY TO SEND?

Without my daughter Avery, there wouldn't be a *Bigs*. She graduated from Vanderbilt University in 2011; however, during her years as a student, Avery hadn't done much to prepare for her future. So at commencement, she received her degree in English and had no idea what to do with it.

For the next eight months, Avery lived at home and with no job in sight, my wife Leigh and I began to worry. But then Avery did something very smart. She sat down and thought about what she had always liked to do and, most importantly, what she was good at.

As a young girl Avery loved acting, but when she discovered that 85% of *professional* actors and actresses are unemployed, she didn't see that as a path to a happy career. Her other passion, and her true talent, was writing. Avery's idea was that she might be able to combine her interest in acting—and talent for writing—in television production. After a focused job search, she received an offer to be the assistant to the co-executive producer of Katie Couric's daytime talk show on ABC. The co-executive producer called Avery personally to tell her the good news and, at the end of that short call, said,

> *Avery, because our show is going live for the first time in a few weeks, I need you to start first thing Monday morning.*

Leigh and I were ecstatic! But our euphoria lasted less than 24 hours when Avery sent us an email with the SUBJECT, *"Is This Okay to Send?"* Addressed to her new boss, it read:

> *Hi Kathy, I can start whenever you need me to but, if possible, I would like to start a week from Monday because that would allow me to tie up some loose ends. I am looking forward to working with you. Best, Avery*

"LOOSE ENDS?. . . A WEEK FROM MONDAY?" As I read that sentence over and over, I felt my heart pounding and my blood pressure rising. I wasn't *mad* at Avery—I was *scared* for her. I knew what was behind her desire to start a week later: she was excited to begin apartment hunting in Manhattan. While I sympathized with Avery's desire to move, when I read her email, my first thought was,

> *Avery's just been offered a job in the BIG LEAGUES and she has no idea what's expected of her!*

In a full-blown panic I responded, *"DO NOT SEND—MORE TO FOLLOW."* Then, on my phone, I began to furiously type a stream-of-consciousness email with 22 bullet points about what I knew Avery needed to understand if she was going to succeed in the work world. These bullet points became the foundation for the original *Bigs,* and what you're reading is a condensed version of that book.

BEFORE THE BIGS

I believe my reaction to Avery's email was heightened by my childhood experiences. The second oldest of five children, I grew up in Lake Forest, Illinois, a beautiful suburb of Chicago. I spent weekends with my extended family on both sides, passed sunshine-filled summers going to camp, and loved playing ice hockey and baseball with my friends. Little did I know that storm clouds were on the horizon and my family was in for some heavy weather.

I was in fourth grade when my father lost his job at Harris Trust. The new position he found was as a plant manager for a small manufacturing company in New Hampshire. That move set the pattern for the next six years; every second year my father would lose his job and our family of seven would pack up and move. After leaving Illinois, I spent fourth and fifth grades in New Hampshire, sixth through eighth in Missouri, before arriving in Massachusetts for ninth grade.

My father didn't keep losing his job because he was dumb or lazy. He was, on the contrary, one of the smartest and hardest-working men I've ever known. The mistake he made was choosing the wrong career. Instead of playing to his strengths in research and numbers, he wanted to manage people.

Unfortunately, my father had little ability to connect with people emotionally, and he was, in fact, quite solitary. These characteristics made it virtually impossible for him to succeed as a manager. The result was a devastatingly painful 30-year working career that ultimately destroyed his confidence. For the family, an air of insecurity permeated every house we rented, and the fear of financial ruin never left us.

However, every time my father was knocked down he, with a great deal of help from my mother, got back up and kept fighting for the family. Despite a steep uphill battle, my parents, to their great credit, were able to send all five of their children to college. I attended Bowdoin College in Brunswick, Maine, and had a great time there. Most importantly, that's where I met my wife Leigh.

FIRST JOB AND MORE

After graduation, I moved to New York City and went to work at Bankers Trust Company in the Empire State Building. My job was to lend money to the fashion industry, which was located in that area of Manhattan. I enjoyed learning about my clients' businesses, but after two years I realized that for my career I wanted more excitement and the opportunity for a larger income. Fortunately, I was able to transfer downtown to the bank's Wall Street trading floor.

For the next three years I sold Treasury bonds, and that job was everything I had hoped it would be. The markets

were exciting. I loved the intense atmosphere of the trading floor, and my income increased. Then I took a similar
job at Morgan Stanley, and a year later I joined a small,
upstart, bond-trading firm in Connecticut, Greenwich Capital, where I stayed for over 20 years.

Greenwich Capital was the scene of my greatest professional successes and failures. When I joined, I was still a
salesman. Then I hit the skids as a trader, before regaining
my footing and eventually becoming the Co-CEO. Similarly,
Greenwich survived some early challenges, but ultimately
became a firm of over 1,200 top professionals and one of
the most respected and profitable firms on Wall Street.

LOOKING BACK

My childhood experiences had a major impact on my career.
From a young age I knew that I wanted to achieve financial
security because money concerns were a constant pressure in our family. I also wanted my children to grow up
feeling that they were part of a community because I
hadn't had that opportunity.

But having to make new friends each time we moved
wasn't all bad—it forced me to develop communication
skills that I've used throughout my career.

FOR YOU

Here are two questions for you to consider.

1. What have been the most important events in your life, and how have they affected who you are?

2. Do you believe these life events could have an impact on your career? How?

Chapter 2

Getting Internships and Jobs

As a senior in college, just like Avery, I knew almost nothing about the professional work world. Therefore, I walked into my first job interview having done no preparation. The position was to be a junior lending officer at J.P. Morgan and the conversation went like this:

Ben, why do you want to be a banker?

I don't know, I was hoping you could tell me about the business.

Not surprisingly, I didn't get the job. But I did receive a wake-up call: my personality and soon-to-be-acquired college degree were not *nearly* enough to get a great job. Today, the race for entry-level jobs has become even more competitive, and you can't afford to stumble out of the starting blocks as I did. For many students, after deciding which fields are of most interest to them, the first step in their professional careers is to apply for internships.

INTERNSHIPS

Back in the Dark Ages, when I was in college, no one I knew had a professional internship—we just had summer jobs. But professional internships are now a fact of life. These internships are important in order to:

- **Explore a particular interest, job, or field** to see if it's right for you.

- **Develop the skills** necessary for the work world.

- **Bolster your resume** by getting experience and showing initiative, determination, and focus in obtaining an internship.

- **Broaden your network** of contacts.

Internships have become so important in preparing for your future that you need to be flexible and creative in seeking them out. Some colleges have long winter or holiday vacations, and students can secure internships during these breaks that they might not be able to get during summers. Another approach is to take a semester off to do an internship, or combine an internship with a study abroad program.

A job doesn't have to be labeled as an internship to provide you and your resume needed experience and credibility. For instance, if you want to work in the hospitality business, being a waiter/waitress in a restaurant, or a housekeeper in a hotel, functions as an internship—though both positions are considered to be traditional part-time or summer jobs. Also, there are many volunteer positions at non-profits which can provide a social good and work experience that are relevant to a wide range of industries.

If you don't know which professional fields might interest you, Chapter 6, Exploring Careers, will help you.

When to Apply for Summer Internships

The process of landing internships and full-time jobs is virtually identical. You need to:

- Decide what field(s) interest you.

- Educate yourself about the field(s).

- Find available internships or jobs.

- Promote yourself as a great candidate for that position.

A mistake many students make is to begin searching for summer internships too late during the school year—these positions are often filled during the fall. When my youngest daughter, Cameron, was a sophomore at Vanderbilt, she applied for a summer internship in September and was told, *"Cameron, congratulations, you're the first student this year to contact us about our summer program."* Now *that's* what you want to hear!

Understanding the academic credentials or qualifications you might need to apply for internships is vital. You can find this information by talking to people who have recently been interns in that industry or organization, or by asking a professional in the Career Services Office of your college.

Understanding the Internship Progression

Two-Year Colleges: If you're attending a two-year college, you should be trying to get an internship after your first year. For you, this first summer functions as a junior year internship at a four-year college, and you may want to skip forward to that section.

Below is the internship progression for four-year college students.

Freshman Year of College: A professional summer internship is not necessary after your freshman year of college. Future potential employers do not expect to see relevant work experience from your freshman-year summer—primarily because so few professional internships are available. Nonetheless, it's a good idea to try to get an internship if you can. How do you do that? For starters, visit your college's Career Services office as soon as possible during your freshman year. Arrange a meeting with a career counselor and tell them what kind of internships you'd like to apply to for that summer.

Even if Career Services can't help you find an internship this summer, hopefully you've established a productive relationship with that counselor. Of course, if you have a strong contact (most likely a parent or a friend's parent) who can get you a summer internship—great!

What *is* important freshman year is to lay the groundwork to get a post sophomore-year internship. It may sound ridiculous to focus on internships a full year forward, but it's essential because sophomore-year internships are scarce. Here are two things you should do as a freshman to prepare for sophomore-year internships:

- **Ask your college's Career Services counselors** what internships they know about for sophomores, and how you can position yourself to get one of those next summer.

- **If you have any family or friend contacts** that might have sophomore-year internships available, talk to them about those internships *now*. If you wait until sophomore year to ask, you run a risk of having someone else grab that precious opportunity before you get your act together.

Sophomore Year of College: During your sophomore year, a professional internship starts to matter. This is because having a sophomore-year internship on your resume can help you attain the most important internship—which is post-junior year.

No later than early fall of your sophomore year you should be using your entire network to identify internships you want and to plan how to get them. While some organizations offer an "open" application process, generally only a small number of positions are available, and many of those are taken by candidates with strong connections inside that company. So muster all the contacts in your network (which are outlined in the next section) and interview for as many internships as possible to increase your chances of obtaining one.

Junior Year of College: This is the big leagues of four-year college internships. Organizations across a wide range of industries offer a substantial percentage of their full-time post-graduation jobs to interns who worked for them the previous summer. Happily, junior internships are much more plentiful than freshman or sophomore ones. Career Services may be able to help you ferret out junior-year internship opportunities, but again, tap any and all of your personal contacts.

If you are talented and fortunate enough to get your dream junior-year internship, aspire to be the *best* intern *ever* at that organization. Possibly no two months of your entire working career will be more important. Dress appropriately *every* day, arrive at work early, ask good questions, and be a good teammate. This is especially important for organizations that use their intern program as the primary feeder system for hiring, because they typically offer 50–75% of their interns a full-time post-graduation job.

During an internship, if you aren't fully engaged each day, come up with ideas on how you can do more. Sometimes it will be appropriate for you to carry out an idea on your own; other times you will need to clear it with your boss. However, avoid always waiting to be told what to do. You need to be proactive and creative. *One of the best sources of ideas for how you can be productive is to ask junior employees at the organization who were recently interns themselves.*

The advice in the Chapter, "How to Do a Great Job," applies as much to interns as it does to full-time employees. Also, first impressions are especially important because most summer internships last 10 weeks or less. Everyone you come into contact with, including other interns, needs to feel positive about you. Although other interns may be competing with you for job offers, you should treat them *all* with consideration and respect. If you're highly regarded by your peers, you will likely be held in high regard by the intern coordinator, who often influences job offers.

Even if your organization does not generally offer interns post-graduation jobs, remember, there can always be exceptions. If you want your internship to turn into a full-time job offer, do an exceptional job and maybe that will happen. If it doesn't, you'll know you did your best, and likely you will have impressed the employees at the organization who will now become valuable members of your professional network.

Post-college internships: Despite my encouragement to focus on getting a job offer before or during senior year, only a modest percentage of students will accomplish that goal. Perhaps you didn't know what you wanted to do, you didn't get an internship, or the organization you worked with did not offer interns full-time jobs.

In fact, 4 out of 5 college students are like Avery and will graduate without a job lined up. If you find yourself in this position, the good news is that you can now focus full-time on getting a full-time position. You may be able to snag a great job by following the advice in *The Bigs.* Or it may make sense to do a post-graduation internship to gain an understanding of a certain field, or to get your foot in the door.

Thank Everyone

Follow up with thank-you notes to all the people you dealt with during your internship. This will increase your chances of getting a full-time job offer at the organization, promote good will if you go work there, or enhance the likelihood of receiving favorable recommendations if you apply for positions elsewhere.

NETWORKING

Now that you understand how internships work, let's examine how to get them *and* how to get jobs. The first step is networking—which might sound complicated but is not. It's simply a fancy name for speaking with professionals about the industry, organization, or job you want. While networking and socializing have many similarities, they are different.

The primary goal of socializing is to have fun. The primary goal of networking is to maximize your career. Networking can help you throughout your professional life, but first we're going to concentrate on how networking can help you get internships and jobs.

Networking is important because over 75 percent of full-time job openings are never advertised, and for internships the percentage is even higher. These internships and jobs are filled by people who find some connection to the hiring firm. Even when good internships and jobs *are* advertised, there will be many, sometimes thousands, of applicants. *The only way to have a realistic chance at getting such an internship or job is to use your network to find someone inside that organization who's willing and able to place your paper or electronic resume at the top of that huge pile—AND put in a good word for you.*

Your Network

Below are the seven primary sources of prospects, also called contacts, which will comprise your network.

1. **Family:** which includes parents, grandparents, god-parents, siblings, uncles, aunts, and cousins. These people aren't first because they necessarily have the best connections. It's because whatever connections your family has, they will work the hardest to maximize them for your benefit. For instance, you may want to work in the field of public health. Your uncle, a fireman, may play softball with the head of the local United Way or he might have gone to school with that person's sister. *You'll never know who-knows-whom until you ask.*

2. **Friends:** as well as their parents, and friends of friends. Any friend, or a friend's parent, who works in your area of interest should be part of your network.

3. **Professors, Counselors, and Coaches:** These are people who have work experience that they can share with you, and sometimes they can introduce you to their former students who work in the field you'd like to explore or enter.

4. **Fellow Students:** if you attend a four-year college, there will be many juniors and seniors who have already gone through the internship and job search process in your field, and they can be invaluable sources of information and contacts. The same is true in community colleges; second-year students are a

great source of career information for first-year students. In fact, some seniors and second-years will already have jobs "in-hand" during their last year in college. Through Career Services or friends, find out who these seniors/second-years are and, whether you know them personally or not, send a short email asking to meet with them to discuss their successful job search. Start doing this as soon as you decide what fields interest you. Then stay in touch with these professionals after they graduate and start their jobs.

5. **Alumni:** You won't have known most of these people, but their allegiance to your school makes it likely that they'll be willing to help you. Virtually all colleges have Career Service offices, and one of their central functions is to provide the database for you to identify alumni who work in your industry. Also, check to see if your high school has a database of professionals from your school.

6. **Co-workers:** at your current or former organizations. For your first job search, this could be co-workers or fellow interns at a company where you interned. For all future job searches, this will be your current and former co-workers. For both Avery and me, these co-worker contacts have been critical in finding great jobs.

7. **LinkedIn:** the professional networking site. LinkedIn can be of immense value in your search to find available internships and jobs, network to be chosen for interviews, and gain the information necessary to excel

in interviews. Also, LinkedIn allows you to post your resume information online. This site is constantly growing and evolving, and becoming adept at using it is a learned skill.

One way to get up to speed quicker is to use your network of friends and family to find active LinkedIn users who are willing to walk you through helpful strategies in your searches for internships and jobs. Another way is to google "LinkedIn power users," where you will find numerous articles on the topic.

You should join LinkedIn *today.* Go to their home page, sign up, create your Profile, and send me an invitation to join your network. Before forwarding your invitation, LinkedIn may ask how you know me. If so, click "Friend." I will accept, and you will then have one "1st degree LinkedIn connection"—me! The good news is that I have over one million 1st and 2nd degree LinkedIn connections that now are your 2nd and 3rd degree connections. As you become more familiar with LinkedIn, you will discover the many ways these connections can help in your searches for internships and jobs.

INFORMATIONAL INTERVIEWS

Landing a great internship/job without preparation is like finding a 10-dollar bill on the sidewalk—it doesn't happen very often. The best way to prepare is through informational interviews—which are a specific form of networking and, therefore, just another fancy name for speaking with professionals about the field, organization, or position you want.

In your internship or job search, the ultimate purpose of networking is to identify openings, attain interviews, and then be hired. However, one of the first steps in preparing for your interviews is to use your network to arrange informational interviews so you can more fully understand the industry, organization, and position you want.

My first job interview was a disaster because I didn't realize that I needed to understand an industry before embarking on job interviews. It was only after I scheduled many informational interviews with Bowdoin College alumni in banking in New York City (where I wanted to live) that I got my first job. It's hard for me to believe how stupid I was back then. And yet, from talking to thousands of job-seekers, I realize that most are no smarter.

When college students come to me for informational interviews, first I congratulate them on realizing the importance of talking to professionals in their field. Second, I ask them how many informational interviews they intend to have. The answer is typically 5–10. When I tell them they should *ultimately* be trying to arrange 40–50 of them, these students invariably look at me with astonishment, and I know they're thinking, *"You've GOT to be kidding."* But I'm not—because informational interviews are critical, and having 40–50 informational interviews will provide you:

- **Education about the industry** so you can have intelligent conversations during job interviews. You can't expect to become an expert, but your goal is to know significantly more about the field and that organization than other candidates applying for the position.

- **Confirmation that the field you think you want to work in is right for you.** Additionally, most have a wide variety of jobs, and it often takes many conversations to understand which position(s) you are best suited for.

- **Practice having professional conversations.** Being confident and persuasive in interviews is a skill that takes time and experience to learn.

- **Exposure to many different professionals and organizations.** I liken searches for internships and jobs to fishing—the more lines you have in the water, the better chance you have to catch something.

Below are the four most important things you need to understand about informational interviews:

#1 Arranging Informational Interviews

While in-person informational interviews are ideal, sometimes they're not feasible, and informational interviews on the phone also work. Below is an example of an email request for an in-person informational interview with a fellow student:

Dear David,

My name is Jack Stevens and I'm a freshman here at UT. Mr. Hartman in Career Services (or a student, coach, or professor) mentioned that after graduation you're going to work as a history teacher in the Springfield school system—congratulations! While I have a ways to go, I'm also planning on becoming a teacher, and I'd love to hear what you learned from your job search. Would you have time for a lunch or coffee? On or off campus, my treat. I would love to meet and hear how you prepared to get this terrific opportunity. Any time or place is good for me.

David, it must feel great to have your job lined up and spring semester to look forward to!

Sincerely,
Jack Stevens

If you do just two of these informational interviews on campus your freshman year, and double that number each year thereafter (2, 4, 8, 16), by the time you graduate you will have done 30 informational interviews and have 30 new professional contacts in your field that you can tap for advice, other contacts, and sometimes internships and job interviews—all without ever leaving campus!

The next sample email is to an alum of your college who works in a field of interest to you:

Dear Ms. Carter,

My name is Kristen Fielding and I'm a sophomore at Maryland. I found your name in the alumni direc-tory. I am extremely interested in pursuing a career in advertising, and I have a particular focus on the account management role. Given your professional background, I would love the opportunity to visit your office to hear your perspective on the business.

I will be in New York from June 4th to June 9th if

that fits your schedule. If not, please let me know what other dates might work. I have attached my resume.

Ms. Carter, thank you for considering this request.

Sincerely,
Kristen Fielding

Among job-seekers, the biggest misperception concerning informational interviews is that they're an imposition on the professional being asked. While some people don't like to do them, my experience is that most professionals enjoy talking about themselves and their careers. During my college campus speaking events, I sometimes highlight this point by asking the students,

After you get started in your career, how many of you would be willing to do informational interviews with students from this college or university looking to enter your field?

Every time I ask that question, virtually every hand goes up.

When you reach out and ask for informational interviews, be happy and grateful when they're granted. If people refuse, or more likely don't respond, don't be discouraged. Use this rejection to fuel your determination to reach out to more people.

As you identify the prospects for your network, and begin having informational interviews, you should keep an electronic file. List the organization, job title, and all contact information concerning that person which is relevant to your job search. After any communication with that person, keep her or his file updated to include the information you just learned—such as the hiring plans of the organization or the names of additional professionals your contact can introduce you to.

#2 Two Extremes of Informational Interviews

While every informational interview is unique, they all fall along a continuum, with the two extremes being:

1. **A true informational interview.** You know little about the field—except that you think that you might like to have an internship or job in it. You are seeking to understand if this field or profession is right for you, and you want to begin educating yourself for future interviews. During these interviews you should ask any and all questions that you have. This type of interview is most appropriate to have with family, fellow students, recent alumni, and professors/counselors/coaches. Below are examples of five good questions to ask during a true informational interview.

   - **Can you tell me about your career** and how you got to this position?
   - **What do you like most about your job?**
   - **Is there a typical career path** for professionals in this field?
   - **What are the best entry-level jobs in this field**, and what qualifications do you need to be considered for them?
   - **How do the most highly regarded people** in this department (or field) achieve that level of success?

2. A job interview in disguise. This means that the interview isn't, from your perspective, actually an informational interview—it's an internship/job interview. You are *not* primarily looking for information; you're looking to impress this contact with your preparation, enthusiasm, and ability to help the organization succeed. Usually, you have this type of interview with senior employees in an organization who could directly influence your getting an internship or job. Optimally, you'd like to have in-disguise interviews *after* you've racked up numerous true informational interviews.

A perfect example of the in-disguise variety was Avery's first and only interview at the *Katie* show. Through a friend of a friend, she had networked to get in touch with the co-executive producer. Avery, via email, asked for an informational interview because she knew the show was about to go on air and felt she could convince the executive producer to hire her. We'll revisit Avery's interview later in this chapter.

#3 Turning Informational Interviews into Job Interviews

Whether it's a true informational interview or one in-disguise, whenever possible, you should try to turn informational interviews into job interviews. There are a number of ways to make this happen. Near the end of an informational interview you can say one or more of the following:

- *Your organization sounds great. Do you know of any internships/job openings I could apply for?*

- *Could you introduce me to someone in your Human Resources (or Personnel) Department?*

- *Do you know any other professionals in this organization, or industry, I might be able to talk to?*

#4 What You Have to Offer

When I explain how informational interviews work, students are often astounded that professionals, most of whom they've never met before, are willing to help them. But this isn't quite the one-way street it appears to be. *You* have something to offer *them*—gratitude.

Kyle Davis, a young Australian who played table tennis for his country at the Beijing Olympics, wanted to work in New York but knew virtually no one there. Someone from the International Olympic Committee gave him a copy of *The Bigs,* and Kyle went all-in. During a lengthy job search he networked his way into having over 70 informational interviews, got his dream job, and opened *my* eyes to the power of gratitude when he explained his process this way:

> *You are trying to get a job, but you need people to help you. They really don't get anything out of it by doing you a favor. But if you are sincerely grateful and able to make them feel special, appreciated, and valued, then they will do whatever they can to help you. Be specific—don't just say thank you—tell them that you appreciate that they were willing to meet and give you such great insights into X, Y, and Z. If you do that, I promise it will make their day!*

OTHER WAYS TO OBTAIN INTERVIEWS FOR INTERNSHIPS AND JOBS

Because such a high percentage of internships and jobs are never advertised, networking and informational interviews should be your primary focus to obtain interviews for available positions. However, that does *not* mean they're the only game in town. Here are two others:

Employment Websites

There are many employment websites with professional job listings. Four of the largest are Monster, CareerBuilder, Indeed.com, and LinkedIn. Many smaller employment websites focus on special industries or jobs, and such sites are constantly being created. Organizations often prefer to list their best internships and jobs on these more specialized sites because they will likely receive fewer resumes from unqualified candidates. Use your network to help you identify the best employment websites for your specific interests.

Once you identify an internship or position that you're interested in, your work has just begun—now use your network to get your resume to the top of the pile.

Career Services

In addition to directories of alumni contacts, most college Career Services offices can also provide leads for specific internships and jobs. In some cases, organizations conduct interviews for internships and jobs on college campuses, and you can sign up at Career Services for these. Often these sign-ups are first come, first serve—so make sure you're first.

INTERVIEWS FOR INTERNSHIPS AND JOBS

Now we're on to the main event. You've used your network and had numerous informational interviews. You've researched your field online. Finally, you've identified an opening for an internship or job through your networking, Career Services, or an employment website, and you've been granted a job interview—Fantastic! You're now ready to ace your interview because few candidates will be as prepared.

The Bigs Cardinal Rule

While necessary, being prepared is not sufficient. You must also know, and abide by, The Bigs Cardinal Rule: *THE INTERVIEW IS NOT ABOUT YOU.*

For example, if you're a musician, athlete, or artist, and that skill doesn't relate to the job opening, you must find ways to connect your talent to personal qualities such as dedication, teamwork, or creativity, which will help *you*— help the *organization* succeed. During an interview, *every* word out of your mouth needs to connect to that message.

THE BIGS TOP 10

The Bigs Top 10 show you how to shine during interviews.

#1 The Wow Factor

Aside from being unprepared, the biggest mistake that young people make during interviews is that they don't show nearly enough enthusiasm. Most interviewees are too timid. They don't realize that being pleasant and qualified will probably *not* land them a highly competitive position.

If you walk out of an interview, and the first thing the interviewer thinks is, *"Nice kid—seemed well qualified,"* you aren't getting that position. Why? Because if it's a good internship or job, there will be *many* nice and well-qualified candidates.

Instead, the interviewer needs to think, *"WOW, that kid is GREAT! I can see her/him at this organization doing an awesome job."* How do you do this? You do your homework so you understand the organization's goals and then show *real* enthusiasm about the position, the firm, and the interview itself.

#2 The Best Preparation

In an interview for an internship or job, the statement below would be extremely effective:

> *I spoke to Mia Jones in your _____ group last week, and she mentioned that _____. I was excited to hear this because of my interest in _____, and it made me even more confident that I could help this organization.*

The secret is to have at least one phone, or in-person, informational interview with someone at the organization *before* your job interview. To find such people, first try the members of your network you know personally and then search your school's alumni network. If you have still found no one, go to LinkedIn because most organizations will have many employees with LinkedIn Profiles. Find the ones you share connections with and send them an email through LinkedIn's InMail—which is a premium feature of LinkedIn, but probably worth the cost during your search for internships and jobs.

For instance, if you have an upcoming interview for an internship with Procter & Gamble (makers of Bounty, Crest, and Tide), and you're a junior at University of Colorado Boulder, LinkedIn lists 40 Profiles of professionals who work for P&G in Denver. Pick out a few of these professionals whom you find some connection with in their Profile or that work in a position similar to the one you'd ultimately like to have, and send them an InMail:

Dear Olivia,

I'm a junior at UC Boulder, and I just found out that next Wednesday I have an interview to be an intern at Procter & Gamble this summer. I discovered your Profile on LinkedIn and I was hoping you might have 10–15 minutes for a call to help me understand more about the company. I also saw that you interned at P&G three years ago and I'd love to hear your thoughts about the program. I've attached my resume.

Olivia, I couldn't be more excited about this interview, and preparing for it is my #1 priority. Thank you for considering this request.

Sincerely,
Emily Moore

Talking to professionals at the organization can give you the inside scoop about the requirements of the position and the type of person they're looking for. These conversations will also allow you to have informed discussions about the organization's culture, new business initiatives, or any other positive information you can glean from employees.

Perhaps most importantly, organizations will assume that the attributes you bring to your search are the same ones you will use on the job. Talking to employees before interviews displays creativity, preparation, networking, and a desire to win. Those skills and attitudes are *exactly* what organizations are looking for.

As an interviewer, I'm impressed whenever I've spoken to candidates who have networked and picked the brains of my co-workers. This relatively easy step will give you a huge advantage because few candidates do it.

Also, if you know who will be interviewing you, research that person online, and especially on LinkedIn, for any shared background (interests, schools, or places you've lived) that could help form a bond, or at least break the ice. In fact, I try to do this before having a professional meeting or phone call with anyone on any issue because it's a great conversation starter to say, *"I saw you played lacrosse, went to Bowdoin College, lived in Missouri, or worked at Bankers Trust—so did I."*

#3 Be General and Specific

During an interview, you may be asked, *"What specific department of this company do you want to work in?"* If you give the response I have heard countless times, *"I don't know . . . I would take any job available,"* you will appear unprepared. Conversely, you shouldn't say, *"I want to work in (a specific) department"* because that department may not be hiring. To walk this tightrope, you might instead say:

> *"I had the chance to talk to Sue Smith in your _____ area, and I also had numerous informational interviews with other professionals in this industry. I believe (insert your specific job interest) would be a great fit for my (specific talents and background). But, there's still a great deal I don't know about this (company or field) and my first goal is to get a job, learn the business, and help the company succeed in any way I can."*

That's an impressive answer. You displayed your preparation for the interview and thought logically about matching your talents and background with your career. You appear practical and flexible, and would focus on helping the organization succeed. Finally, you left the door open to be a candidate for any entry-level job openings—all in three sentences!

Similarly, be prepared to answer the questions: *"Why do you want to work at this organization?"* and *"Why do you want to work in this field?"* As with the answer to which department you want to work in, the best responses will highlight conversations you have had with employees of that organization or other professionals in that industry.

#4 Show Confidence

As her interview with the co-executive producer of the *Katie* show began, Avery was excited because this was her dream job. Near the middle of the conversation, however, the woman said, *"Avery, I really like you, but I want you to know that the show is fully staffed and there aren't any jobs available."* Avery knew the interview had been going well and, because of that, this statement was a punch in the stomach.

Outwardly, though, Avery stayed positive. At the end of the interview, as they were shaking hands, Avery said, *"It's been great talking to you and, if you give me a chance, I know I can help make this new show a success."*

That evening over dinner, when Avery was describing her interview, she related that when she delivered that final line, the co-executive producer looked startled—as if she were thinking, *"Did this girl really just say that?"* But while not expecting any job offer, Avery was glad she had said it because, in her words, *"It was the truth."* Two weeks later when Avery received the job offer, the first thing she told me was, *"I think I got it because of what I said at the end."* I think that Avery's probably right.

#5 Putting It All Together

It's easier to show confidence and enthusiasm if you've already thought about answers to questions you might be

asked. Below are five of the most common interview questions. Imagine that I just graduated from college and you're
interviewing me for a position.

Question 1: What can you tell me about yourself?
Because my father had an unsuccessful business career,
my family moved every couple of years—often halfway
across the country—to wherever he found his next job. I
was always the "New Kid" and I constantly had to make
new friends. Though at times it was painful, I now realize that I was developing some good communication
skills and I learned to be resilient.

Question 2: What are your greatest weaknesses? I can
be too much of a risk taker. For instance, when I first got
my driver's license in high school I often drove reck-
lessly. Around the same time, my buddies and I used to
find places to jump off high rock ledges and bridges into
the rivers. Sometimes we didn't know how deep the
water was, and I always wanted to go first. That stuff
was stupid and I've outgrown it. But I think it shows a
desire for risk-taking that I'm aware I need to control.

Question 3: How can you help this organization succeed?
My biggest asset is persistence. Seeing my father fail in
his professional career made me determined to succeed. I'm not a great natural athlete, but that hunger for
success made me an overachiever. I was elected captain
of my college lacrosse team and became a New England
All-Star—after not playing the sport until my junior year
of high school. I'm even *more* hungry for professional
success because that can earn me the financial security
my family never had.

Question 4: What are your goals? Ultimately, I want to run a department or a business. As an athlete, I liked to score goals, but more than that I loved helping the team win. I've always gotten the greatest kick out of making the play that allowed someone else to score, and then seeing the huge smile on their face. *That's* what I enjoyed most about playing team sports.

Question 5: What do you like to do for fun? I have to admit, once again, it's sports. Since lacrosse ended, I'm starting to play golf. I love the feeling when I occasionally crush a drive. But the thing I like *most* about golf is spending four hours competing and being with friends.

I'm sure some of you just read my answers and said to yourself, *"That's no help to me, I've lived my whole life in one town and I'm not very into sports."* In fact, that describes Avery perfectly. But Avery was able to give similar answers to these same types of questions. She simply substituted *her* talent in theater and writing—which had allowed her to win acting roles and public speaking awards—for *my* interest in sports. Doing this enabled her to tell a *great* story about how she could help a company in *her* industry.

#6 Selling Your College Major

A question I often hear from college students is, *"What I'm studying in college doesn't directly relate to the career I'm considering—is that okay?"* My short answer is a definitive *"Yes."* But you will probably need to explain why you chose the major you did and how the skills it taught you relate to the position you want.

Being prepared to sell your major is especially important for liberal arts students. Remember, the primary purpose of these majors is to teach you how to think. So part of selling a liberal arts degree should be, *"From my studies, I've learned how to learn. Give me a problem to solve and I'll quickly figure out the answer—by talking to experts, by researching online, or both."*

When I was a college senior interviewing for my first full-time job, I can't remember if I was challenged about why I had majored in Government and wanted to be a banker. But if I had been, this would be a good answer:

> *At Bowdoin, I have loved studying the strengths and weaknesses of different forms of government, and how the governments of different countries operate. Fundamentally, governments and companies are both trying to manage people, and I believe that the general skills I've developed researching and analyzing countries can be applied to companies. But I do understand that there's a great deal of finance-specific knowledge I need to learn, and that's why I'm excited about your commercial lending training program.*

Looking back, I'm certain I wouldn't have come up with an answer nearly that good because I didn't have anyone coaching me. You, however, do. If your career choice doesn't clearly match your academic studies, be sure to have your personal version of my college-major explanation all warmed up and ready to go.

As you practice that pitch, remember that for your explanation to be convincing *you* must believe in it— because the truth is always the easiest thing to sell.

Last, if you have an idea of what career(s) interest you, and they don't directly relate to your major, it's a good idea to have a minor (mine was economics), or take courses, that are relevant to your career interests.

#7 Two Questions You Will Be Asked

Having just had 70 informational interviews, Kyle Davis, the Aussie table tennis player, became an expert at what questions you will be asked, and he guarantees that the first question in any interview is, *"How are you?"* Kyle recommends that you return serve:

> *Don't say "good" and wait for the next question. There is no warm-up in an interview for an internship or job. The game has begun and the best answer is, "I'm great thank you, how are you?" You just expressed enthusiasm, gratitude, interest in the interviewer, and confidence by asking a question. Now THAT'S a perfect way to be begin an interview.*

Towards the end of an internship/job interview, you can generally tell when the interviewer wants to conclude the conversation when she/he asks, *"Do you have any more questions for me?"* Usually when I ask this question of job candidates, there's an awkward pause, followed by a vague, *"Nooo, I think I understand . . ."* Don't lose the positive energy you've worked so hard to create! This is a great time to reemphasize your preparation by, without hesitation, responding,

> No, not really, but from my research about this company online, my discussions with Bill Smith and Ann Walker in your _____ department, and this interview with you, I feel I have a solid understanding of this firm and I know I could do a great job at the position you're looking to fill.

This question provides the opportunity for you to "close strong," which is important because the last thing you say in an interview will be the first thing an interviewer remembers when you walk out the door.

#8 Who's In Charge?

In an interview for an internship or job, it's *your* responsibility to make sure that the conversation touches on all the strongest points about you as a candidate. The interviewer already has a job, but this half hour is *your* shot to get an internship or job.

If the interviewer asks questions that allow you to make all your points—great! If not, while being respectful, you need to take charge by interjecting, *"There are a couple of things I wanted to mention about. . . ."* During an interview, you *can't* afford to be passive and leave it up to the interviewer to decide if you're the right person. You need to *convince* the organization to hire you, and you may need to take charge of this important moment to do that effectively.

#9 What To Ask and Not To Ask

Questions to ask during interviews must reflect your enthusiasm and preparation. Below are two examples of this:

- *I've had a wonderful time talking to many people in this field, and I keep hearing positive things about your organization's _____. Why have you been so successful with this?*

- *I read in your company's annual report that you're looking to expand into South America. I'm not aware of any of your competitors doing this. What's the opportunity you see in the region?*

These two questions are quite different from the five we looked at for true informational interviews. Here, you aren't really looking for information—you're making a sales pitch for yourself in the form of a question.

Also, remember to ask the interviewer at least one question about their specific job and/or career. If you're speaking to someone in Human Resources whose job it is to interview candidates, you can ask, *"How did you come to work at XYZ company?"*

Questions you should NEVER ask during interviews for internships and jobs concern salary, benefits, working conditions, hours, promotions, or any negative issues concerning the organization. As things progress, hopefully after receiving a job offer, you can ask those questions.

If you're looking to switch positions, you will often be asked what you didn't like about your previous one. Look out for that question—it's a trap. *In an interview you should never be negative about anything.* While interviewing, you should always say your previous job, boss, or career was good, but you are even *more* excited about this new opportunity.

#10 When To Arrive and What To Wear

You need to show professional consideration for your interviewer by arriving 5–10 minutes early. The way to ensure this is to give yourself enough travel leeway that only a natural disaster could make you late. Given the time you've allowed, normally, you will be outside the organization with much more than 10 minutes to spare, but don't go in. Take a walk or sit on a bench: you want to arrive on time, but not too early.

The rule for what to wear for interviews is: *DRESS AT LEAST ONE NOTCH BETTER THAN THE EMPLOYEES AT THE ORGANIZATION.* If the organization is "business casual," which for men is slacks, button-down shirt, and sometimes a blazer, you dress business formal: blue or gray suit and tie. If male employees wear cargo shorts and t-shirts, you dress business casual.

According to Avery and Leigh, business formal for women is often a black or navy skirt or pants suit, a conservative top, low heel pumps or flats, simple accessories, and only modest amounts of jewelry. Business casual for women varies greatly. So, unless you are certain what appropriate dress is at an organization, your interview outfit should always be business formal.

I've been asked by students, *"I love fashion, can't I dress a little hipper than that?"* If the industry you're looking to enter is intensely creative or is specifically in the fashion business, you can be a little more edgy because your fashion sense directly relates to the job you want.

For most companies and jobs, however, to dress overtly fashionably is not a good idea. Why? Because, some interviewers will feel that you're breaking the Cardinal Rule of Interviewing—*THIS IS NOT ABOUT YOU*—and it can detract from your primary message, which is, *"I'm looking for the opportunity to help your organization accomplish its goals."*

When interviewing, make certain that your entire presentation—how you act, what you say, and how you look—stays aligned with the Cardinal Rule.

STUDYING ABROAD

Most of the 300,000 U.S. college students who study abroad each year do so for one semester during their junior year. If you are in that group, you may need some additional planning concerning your summer internship. Different intern programs have different schedules, and if you will be away when you need to apply or interview, contact those organizations and explain your situation. Since being abroad may also hinder your ability to have informational interviews, do as many of those as possible *before* you leave.

POSTGRADUATE DEGREES

In the future, some of you will consider a postgraduate degree. I am hugely enthusiastic about acquiring additional education if it's needed to accomplish your career goals.

What I *don't* recommend, however, is getting a postgraduate degree in order to figure out what you want to do. For most people, the out-of-pocket and foregone income expenses are too high to attend graduate school just to find their way. That's one of the things informational interviews are for.

I never got a postgraduate degree because I didn't need it in my career, but I have many friends who went to business school and swear by it. In addition to its being a necessary credential for some positions, MBA enthusiasts often assert that it's impossible to quantify the value of the personal and professional connections they made at business school.

FOLLOWING UP

One of the least fun parts of an internship/job search is following-up, and most jobseekers fall short here. But getting a job *is* a job and, as you know from being a student, not every part of every task is enjoyable. However, following up is critical and it includes:

1. **Sending two more email requests for an interview** if the first one is overlooked or ignored.

2. **Immediately writing thank-you notes after all interviews.** They should be two paragraphs that: thank the person for taking the time, mention one interesting part of the conversation, and confirm that you will follow up on specific topics discussed.

3. **Sending second and third email follow-ups, after the interview and initial thank-you note**, to keep in touch

with that person—with the hopes that a job opportunity or referral might turn up after your interview. For Human Resources professionals, stay in touch once a month. For all others, once every three to four months is appropriate. Below is an example of such an email:

Dear Ms. Smith,

My search for an internship in health care administration has continued to progress well. I haven't yet achieved my goal of securing a position for this summer, but I know I'm making headway. From speaking to professionals like you, my excitement about the industry has grown.

Ms. Smith, thank you for taking time to talk with me. If you can think of others I should speak to, I would love to make those contacts.

Sincerely,
James Garcia

4. **After getting your great position**, sending a thank-you note to *everyone* whom you interviewed with or *anyone* who helped you in any way. This is both common courtesy and very much in your self-interest. These people were your best contacts and you may well end up working with, or for, some of these professionals in the future. Also, it's likely this job will not be your last and you may need help from these folks in your next job search.

Finally, receiving a thank-you note will make these professionals more likely to help the next person who asks—who might be a friend or relative you're trying to help by sharing your industry contacts. I prefer email because it's easier to read and respond to, but some people like handwritten notes. Whichever you choose, it should say something similar to:

Dear Ms. Smith,

I am writing to thank you again for speaking to me about the marketing industry and to tell you the good news—I got a job! The company is Jack Morton Worldwide and I will be an events planner here in their Boston office.

I am grateful to you for the time you spent with me. Your insights and advice were extremely helpful in getting me up to speed. Without your help, I wouldn't have been as prepared to compete for this great opportunity.

Ms. Smith, below is my new contact information. I hope to see you soon, either professionally or perhaps at a Boston College alumni event. Thank you again!

Sincerely,
Emma Bryant

Everyone likes to be thanked and everyone enjoys hearing good news, so use this happy occasion of getting a job to strengthen your network. I know that receiving such an email always makes me smile and want to help that person—and others—in the future.

A CLOSER LOOK AT NETWORKING

My network was critical in helping me get my first job, but it didn't stop there. It's not an exaggeration to say that my network *was* my career. It both got me started and kept me going, and this is quite typical.

- **First**, my college's Career Services office suggested I look into banking.

- **Second**, informational interviews with alumni from my college educated me about the business.

- **Third**, my first contact with Bankers Trust came through my mother—who worked at a school where one of the parents was a lending officer at Bankers.

- **Fourth**, at Bankers, when I wanted to move from commercial lending to the trading floor, a classmate from the lending training program, who had already made that move, helped me do the same.

- **Fifth**, when I was looking to join Morgan Stanley, part of the reason I was an attractive candidate was because senior managers at Morgan Stanley respected Bankers Trust.

- **Sixth**, when I was looking to move from Morgan Stanley, it was a friend from Bankers, now working at Greenwich Capital, who called me.

- **Seventh**, while I was a salesman at Greenwich, my old boss from Bankers became my client.

- **Eighth**, when I became a manager at Greenwich, I hired dozens of my ex-colleagues from Bankers and Morgan Stanley.

And those are just the highlights. Most of the positive events that occurred during my career have been the result of personal relationships developed inside or outside the office. *As an employee, doing high quality work will put you in position for good things to happen, but how people FEEL about you will significantly determine the opportunities that come your way.*

FOR YOU

Here are four questions for you to consider.

1. Have you spoken to your family, or other professionals, about their jobs and how they got them?

2. Have you thought about getting an internship or job and who in your network might be able to help you? Who would be the first five on your list?

3. How would you try to present your interests, talents, and accomplishments as something that could help an organization succeed?

4. Have you had interviews for internships or jobs? What do you think you did well, and what could you improve?

Chapter 3

Starting a Business

When I graduated from college and moved to New York City, there were only two things I was trying to accomplish: I wanted to learn how to be a banker, and I wanted to keep having fun. As luck would have it, soon after I moved into my apartment, I joined a softball team that was sponsored by a local bar which was very popular with young professionals. One night while still in my uniform, as I stood at the bar celebrating our latest victory, I looked around at the boisterous crowd and thought,

> *I could do this . . . I could get all these people to come to MY bar!*

But there were two problems: I didn't own a bar and I had almost no money. However, *I did have a good idea and, in business, that's THE most important thing.*

The next evening, having spent the day writing credit reports for Bankers Trust, I traded in my suit and tie for a T-shirt, jeans, and sneakers, and headed out into my neighborhood on the Upper East Side in search of a bar that needed more customers.

After a pleasant stroll, the very first watering hole I saw that looked promising was a one-story building on the corner of 89th and First Avenue. On the front window, in crudely-painted chipped and faded lettering, was the name of the bar.

TUMBLE INN

From the outside, Tumble Inn was the most beat-up, run-down, and forlorn-looking bar I'd ever seen on the East Side and it didn't get any better when I opened the door. The inside looked like a movie set for a film about the Great Depression, and the three people in the bar—two old men slumping on stools and a slightly younger white-haired woman behind the bar—looked perfectly cast for the picture. Time and grime had conspired to turn everything a dark gray. I quickly came to understand that the bartender owned this august establishment.

Margie

With her snow-white hair and strong personality, Margie provided the only color in the place. She was in her late 50's and maybe five feet tall. She had been a bartender at the Tumble Inn for most of her working life, and took the place over from the previous owner. Having grown up in the neighborhood, Margie had a classic New York in-your-face personality and the accent to go with it. After we got to know each other, she would preface all verbal communication to me by barking rapidly *"Ben-Ben-Ben"* and then telling me whatever was on her mind.

I don't remember what Margie and I talked about that first night, but after a few beers and a round for the house (big spender), I walked back to my apartment with a spring in my step, smiling and thinking, *"This is gonna be GREAT!"* One thing I failed to notice on that first visit was a single, but large and unmistakable, bullet hole in the plexiglas window just above the bar's name.

The next night I brought Leigh down to see what she thought of my new "find." Aside from thinking Margie was kind of cute, the only comment Leigh had about my plan was, *"Have you lost your mind?"* While I knew Leigh was smarter than me about most things, I believed strongly in my idea and had a clear vision of what the Tumble Inn could become.

After a few more solo visits, I asked Margie about the lease and whether she was interested in being partners. Since my subsequent visits to the bar confirmed that the Tumble Inn was in *desperate* need of more customers, Margie *was* interested. Also, she told me the good news: Tumble Inn had more than seven years left on its lease and the rent was quite cheap.

Since I had barely three nickels to rub together (my salary from the bank was already spoken for in rent and slices of pizza), I had to devise an attractive offer for Margie that didn't involve cash. What I came up with was simple but perfect.

First, all bills would be paid—which included rent, utilities, beer, liquor, and bartenders. Second, Margie would be paid a salary for managing the bar—which was more than she was currently making. Third, Margie and I would split the remaining money equally.

While my idea earned me a free half-share of the bar, I did have to empty my meager bank account to ready the Tumble Inn for the big leagues. I didn't have the cash, or desire, to change the aesthetics of the bar, but I did invest in stereo equipment for a DJ and a big TV for the ballgames. Then I put handwritten mimeographed flyers under hundreds of apartment doors in the neighborhood and word-of-mouth began to spread the news.

After my softball team switched allegiance and a few friends had private parties, and with the best college-style DJ in town amping up the energy, the Tumble Inn took off like a rocket and seemingly nothing could stop us!

Some of my favorite memories from those early days were when the place was rockin' and Margie would go behind the bar and put on her show. With her new clientele packed together like a circus crowd too large for the tent, pushing forward and screaming for more beer, Margie performed like a lion tamer—yelling, swearing, and generally treating these young professionals like the wild animals they were at that moment. With her scrappy New York personality, this was a role Margie was born to play, and both the star and her audience loved the show.

Tough Guys

There are always surprises when you begin a new venture, and those surprises are seldom pleasant. In the case of the Tumble Inn, the surprise was the reemergence of the bar's previous clientele.

While nobody *"knew nuttin"* about the bullet hole in the front window, after I got to know the old Tumble Inn patrons, I quickly realized it could have been fired by—or at—any of them. Being on the northern edge of the Upper East Side, the neighborhood around the Tumble Inn was dicey. To the immediate south gentrification was in full swing. To the north, however, was a tough, old-time New York neighborhood, and some of its residents—the Tough Guys—used to call the Tumble Inn home.

The first few months after the new Tumble Inn opened were a dream. Packed to the rafters every Thursday, Friday, and Saturday night, it was the place to be for young professionals. But then the Tough Guys decided they wanted in on the fun. Margie knew all the Tough Guys, but they were used to her screaming and didn't care much about anything she had to say.

Our two groups of patrons did not mix—except to fight. Suddenly, the Tumble Inn became a Wild West saloon with Tough Guys and Preppies alternately being thrown out the front door onto First Avenue, picking themselves up, and rushing back in for more.

Quickly, things shifted from bad to near-disaster. Friends, and friends of friends, were having pool cues and bottles broken over their heads, and general mayhem was the order of the day. More than once, as I was putting on my suit and tie to go to work at Bankers Trust, I looked in the mirror and saw I was sporting a black eye from a melee at the bar. Business began to slow down, but what concerned me most was the growing realization that eventually someone in the Tumble Inn was going to be seriously injured—or worse.

I tried everything I could think of to stop the fights. I played peacemaker, but after enough alcohol neither Preppies nor Tough Guys were swayed by words or logic. I hired a massive bouncer, but after the first night he quit, saying, *"No job and no amount of free beer is worth getting killed for."* I considered hiring off-duty police to keep law and order, but decided they would probably shut down the bar due to our innumerable building code violations.

Just as I was running out of ideas, Leigh came to the rescue. While she initially had been unenthusiastic about the Tumble Inn, she now realized what a huge success it had become. Not wanting the bar—or me—to fail, Leigh told me how to get rid of the Tough Guys: *"Raise the price of Tumble Inn beer."*

I blurted out, *"No way. We're supposed to be an inexpensive dive bar."* However, the Tumble Inn had become more of a nightclub than a neighborhood bar, and desperate times require desperate measures. So after a brief discussion with Margie, the price of beer jumped 30%.

As Leigh had predicted, the Tough Guys quickly decided that Tumble Inn beer was now too expensive and left to fight somewhere else. The Preppies didn't care how much the beer cost as long as it was cold and there were lots of other Preppies to drink with, and Margie and I happily sold more suds at much higher prices. If only all business problems could be solved so simply, effectively, and profitably!

With the Tough Guys crisis resolved, and our establishment no longer doubling as the local Octagon, business exploded. Tumble Inn was a nightclub without a cover charge, velvet rope, or any other pretensions. You went there if you wanted to go crazy with friends and hear great tunes blasted by a great DJ. Most young professionals who were in Manhattan from 1981 to 1988 experienced the rough charms of our bar. Over the years, when I meet new people, I've been told countless times, *"You're the guy who did the Tumble Inn . . . that place was wild . . . I met my wife/husband there!"*

Six Lessons from the Tumble Inn

While the Tumble Inn was a for-profit business, the lessons from it also apply to non-profits. As you read these lessons, think about how you might apply them to ideas you've had.

1. **The most valuable asset is a great idea.** Until that one night after the softball game, I *never* considered owning *any* bar. I had just moved to New York, was beginning my career in banking, and wasn't looking for any outside projects. However, an idea occurred to me, I investigated it, came up with a plan, and by putting one foot in front of the other, made the idea become a reality. Similarly, before Avery sent the *"Is This Okay to Send"* email, I had never thought of writing a book

2. **If you don't have money, don't worry.** If you have a great idea, and can sell your ability to execute your business plan, there's *always* money available. In the case of the Tumble Inn, not having cash wasn't an issue because the bar was sinking and my idea was a lifeboat. A more typical situation is for an entrepreneur to raise funds from family, friends, or outside investors. Regardless of the specific circumstances,

lack of money should *never* be a reason to stop pursuing an entrepreneurial idea.

3. **You need an edge.** One of the first questions smart business veterans ask about any new venture is, *"what's your edge?"* This is shorthand for, *"What's so compelling about your product or service that customers are going to want to buy it from you and not from your competitors?"*

   In the case of the Tumble Inn, my edge (in addition to finding a failing bar in a good location with a long-term lease) was knowing exactly what my clients wanted and having the ability to reach them directly and cheaply with guerrilla marketing (which means accessing your target audience through word-of-mouth, flyers, or any form of inexpensive direct or electronic contact).

   This is why it's likely that most of your successful entrepreneurial ideas will come from industries you know well and/or whose products or services are sold to customers similar to you.

4. **Expect the unexpected.** In any new business venture, many unforeseen problems will crop up. Sometimes these can't be overcome, and other times the sun breaks through. Leigh solved my Tough Guys problem, but the experience taught me to expect the unexpected. This is an important lesson for your business planning *and* your mental health.

5. **Cash is the oxygen that keeps companies alive.** Because business is so unpredictable, always plan for

a worst-case scenario by keeping your expenses as low as possible. This may sound obvious, but tolerating avoidable expenses is an all-too-common reason why many businesses go under. Running a tight ship on expenses helped the Tumble Inn stay afloat during the slow down induced by the Tough Guys, and later it maximized the bar's profitability.

6. **Be creative.** My response to the brawls in the Tumble Inn was conventional—I hired a bouncer. But it was Leigh's unconventional idea to raise prices that saved the business.

WHAT LEADS THE PARADE

After I had been working my two jobs—at Bankers Trust and Tumble Inn—for about a year, my sales manager, Pat Alexander, came by my desk late one afternoon and sat down next to me.

Pat: *How you doin' Ben?*

Me: *Okay I guess.*

Pat: *You don't seem okay to me.*

Me: *What?*

Pat: *Ben, you're dead on your feet and I'm not the only one to notice. What's going on?*

Me: *Well, you know, I got this bar and—*

Pat: *Is the BAR more important to you than this JOB?*

Me: *Well no, but—*

Pat: *THEN GET SOME GODDAMN SLEEP!*

As I watched Pat walk away, I sat there stunned. He was a highly respected and even-keeled leader on the trading floor, and I had never heard him yell at anyone. While the Tumble Inn continued to be my primary outside activity, I significantly cut back on my weeknight hours there.

I was fortunate that Pat gave me a second chance, but the lesson here is *enormously* important: Regardless of whatever interests and obligations you have (family, school, sports, hobbies, charities, or a second job), your full-time boss expects your full-time commitment. If you forget what leads the parade, your career prospects are certain to deteriorate, and you run the risk of not being allowed to march with the band—or maybe being thrown off the float!

WHEN AND HOW TO BE AN ENTREPRENEUR

For many people, the answer to "when" is never. To be an entrepreneur you need a high tolerance for risk and a great idea. The idea can be for a new product or service, or a way to provide an existing product or service better or cheaper.

If you do have a tolerance for risk and you have a great idea, you're in the game. But to start a new business successfully you'll also need a good market for your product, good employees, good financial backing, tenacity, and some good luck.

The timing of when to start your business will be dictated by when all these requirements merge. However, *it's generally a good idea to get some business experience before trying to swim in the treacherous waters of full-time entrepreneurship.*

To the question of "how," one alternative to being a full-time entrepreneur is part-time—which is how I managed the Tumble Inn. You're still competing in the same free market that's equally demanding for all; however, the personal risks of failure are much less because you have the safety net of your full-time job.

I know many people who have taken the plunge to start a company later in their careers when the risk to their financial security was modest. By then they had acquired the expertise, track record, and contacts needed to attract the big money and top talent that's sometimes necessary for new ventures.

FOR YOU

Here are three questions for you to consider:

1. Do you think being an entrepreneur is for you? Why?

2. Have you ever had a great idea for a new business? What made you think of it? Why did you love the idea?

3. What do you need to make this idea happen?

Chapter 4

Doing a Great Job

L ost in the excitement of searching for internships and jobs, or starting a business, the topics of how to do a great job and leadership are often neglected. But what's the point of getting an internship or job, or opening a business, if you're not going to maximize that opportunity?

Of the 22 bullet points I sent to Avery, 9 were specific to being an executive assistant, but the others apply to most positions. Below you'll find the universal bullet points reprinted in their original form. Every time I read these, I flash back to the fear I felt for my daughter that day.

MY ADVICE TO AVERY

- ***Don't strive to do a good job; strive to do an outstanding job.*** You're not going to be an assistant forever, but the impression you make on your boss could well have an impact on your entire career. This is an incredible opportunity, so make the most of it. You want your boss to believe you're the best assistant in the entire world.

- **Consistency of effort and actions is critical.** As a student, nobody expected you to be on your game 100% of the time. As a full-time employee, however, that *is* expected. If your effort or actions are subpar just 1% of the time, that 1% is all anyone will remember when they think about your job performance.

- **Meet all deadlines.** One basic requirement for doing an outstanding job is to handle all your work-related tasks, large or small, in a timely manner. If your job is to finish a report by Friday, finish it by Friday. If Human Resources asks you to fill out a form today, do it today.

- **Don't ever complain to anyone in the company about your job.** If it gets back to your boss, she will think it unprofessional and wonder why you didn't talk to her directly. I hope this position will be awesome, but if it isn't, you need to keep a positive attitude, do a great job, and at the earliest possible time transfer into a job you want.

- **Always get to work earlier and stay later than your boss.**

- **Initially do a lot more listening than talking.** If your boss wants to engage in a discussion of your ideas, then go for it. However, unless she asks for your opinion, you should focus on understanding what she wants you to do and then doing it—brilliantly! There will be plenty of time in the future to assert yourself and share your ideas.

- *If your boss takes you along to meetings* (fingers crossed), you should say afterwards, *"Thank you for including me; I learned a lot."* You don't need to say this repeatedly, but if you acknowledge that she's going out of her way to help you learn, she will be more likely to keep inviting you.

- *Quickly find one or more mentors* or peers who can answer your questions and show you the ropes. Also, observe how the star performers in your office do their jobs. Imitate their best traits, and be creative in figuring out how to do an even better job.

- *If you find you don't have the skills needed* to accomplish some task, such as creating spreadsheets or reports, don't fake it. Speak up immediately and find out how and where to learn the skill. Don't wait until it becomes a major problem. When you start, your boss will not expect you to know everything, but in three months she will.

- *When you make mistakes, quickly own up to them.* Apologize, correct the problem, and move on.

- *Regularly ask yourself one question: "If I were my boss, am I doing everything the way I would want it done?"*

- *Never say anything negative about your co-workers.* Assume anything you say about anyone will get back to them. Follow this *"golden rule"* both inside and outside the company. You never know who might say what to whom, and we all know it can be a *very* small world.

- ***Don't be scared.*** You're an incredible young woman and more than capable of doing this job exceptionally well. You will, however, need to work hard, be disciplined and, most of all, pay attention!

SO, WHAT HAPPENED?

Many people ask, *"So, what happened to Avery? Did she start work that first Monday?"*

Being a parent, I'm accustomed to my ideas not being treated as gospel, and that was part of my panic: I didn't know if Avery was going to listen to me. Thankfully she did. First, she *did not* send the *"Is This Okay to Send?"* email, and she *did* start work that Monday. Second, Avery adhered to all the bullet points that proved relevant to her job and the work environment at ABC, but one in particular stood out.

Avery's position required her to arrive at work by 7 AM to scour the overnight wire services for news that might be of interest to the Katie show. The rest of the office, and her boss, arrived at 9 AM. The catch was that while everyone else left around 6 PM, Avery's boss stayed until 9 PM.

Having been told to *"arrive earlier and stay later"* than her boss, Avery—without being asked—did just that. Within a few months, Avery's boss, as if quoting the first bullet point, was telling people at the studio that she had *"the best assistant ever."* Eight months later, Avery received a much earlier-than-expected promotion to join one of the production teams.

The epilogue to this story is that after the *Katie* show ended its two-year run, Avery's newly expanded network kicked in and a former producer from the show referred Avery to a rapidly growing daily email newsletter, *The Skimm,* which summarizes each day's current events in a brief and entertaining format. Avery is now one of the two lead writers of *The Skimm* and loves her job.

It's impossible to know which of the bullet points will be most important to your specific position and work environment; however, "My Advice to Avery" applies to virtually ALL positions, at ALL organizations, ALL the time.

FOR YOU

Here are three questions for you to consider.

1. When have you been challenged to do your very best at something? How did you respond?

2. Which bullet points do you believe are most important?

3. Because of your strengths and weaknesses, which bullet points do you need to pay special attention to?

Chapter 5

Being a Leader

Right off the bat, you can be a leader your very *first* day on the job. You're probably thinking, *"How's that possible? I'll be the lowest rung on the ladder!"* The answer is that the foundation for all leadership is to lead by example—which isn't easy, but it's also not complicated. The previous chapter told you most of what you need to do, and it was summarized in the first bullet point: *"Don't strive to do a good job; strive to do an outstanding job."*

Surprisingly, during my 35-year working career I can count only a few co-workers who consistently lived up to that standard. Most employees strive to do a good job, but what they don't understand is that they were hired, and they're being paid, to do a good job. *Therefore, doing a good job is the bare minimum of acceptable performance.*

If you want to be identified as someone the organization will give outsized opportunities and compensation to, you must do an outstanding job. In practical terms, this means arriving early, doing what's assigned to you with diligence and energy, and most importantly, *constantly* looking for ways to help your co-workers and organization succeed.

Some of the information and advice in this chapter is important for you to know now, and some will apply in the near future. All of it, however, will help you achieve your professional goals.

WHEN TO PUT YOUR INTERESTS SECOND

Most employees—junior and senior—believe that the key to being promoted is having a great relationship with their boss. While that can be helpful, it's much more important to have a great relationship with everyone else in your office. Why? Because how your boss regards you as a professional will, ultimately, be determined by how everyone else feels about you.

For example, if your boss loves you, but your co-workers don't, it's difficult for your boss to promote you into a management position. However, if you don't have a close relationship with your boss, but your co-workers love you, it's difficult for your boss *not* to promote you. Remember, everyone in your office is important—from the security guard to the CEO.

The best way to have a great relationship with your co-workers is to put your interests *second* to theirs. While this can sometimes be difficult, it's all about taking the long view. *If you give support and credit to others, you'll be surprised by how quickly your co-workers want you to be elevated to a leadership position.*

A closely related issue is my "golden rule" from the

previous chapter: *"Never say anything negative about your co-workers."* One time I broke this rule by bad-mouthing a department head to one of his subordinates. Predictably, the subordinate relayed my comment to his boss and it nearly sank my career. How do you avoid this torpedo? Anytime you are around co-workers who are speaking ill of others, remove yourself from the discussion. If you're put on the spot and asked what you think of a person whom you might not like, just say, *"I don't really know him/her all that well."* Rising above negativity at work will distinguish you from most other employees, and will significantly increase your chances of ending up on top.

WHEN TO PUT YOUR INTERESTS FIRST

While you should be generous and put your interests *second* in the office, you must always put your interests *first* regarding where you work. *If you're in a job that won't allow you to achieve your hopes and dreams, you must move—quickly.* It's easier to switch fields, organizations, and jobs when you're young, and it's also easier to take career risks then because you're less likely to have other people depending on your income.

This is something I was pretty good at. I was always looking, and willing, to move for a better opportunity. However, as Leigh constantly and correctly reminds me, my weakness is that I often don't fully investigate my ideas before jumping in. The lesson here is that you must be impatient—yes, *impatient*—but also thoroughly research all possible career moves before diving in.

NEGOTIATING

The ability to negotiate is a valuable skill you can use today as a student and tomorrow as a professional. Two examples of major commitments you might need to negotiate currently are buying a car or signing a lease for housing.

Negotiating is something I'm *not* naturally good at. I'm a successful manager because I approach issues with a reflexive desire to find the fairest outcome for all involved. In negotiating, however, the goal is to achieve the *best* outcome for yourself or your organization—with little regard for the other side—unless you're addressing a long-term business relationship such as with a vendor or client.

Despite its not being a strength, I've learned a great deal about negotiating from being a bar owner, a Wall Street CEO, and a partner with Leigh making decisions for our family. The following are five hard-earned lessons about how to be an effective negotiator.

1. **Have alternatives.** Having your heart set on one thing is weakness; having options is strength. For instance, whenever I've looked to make a significant purchase, personally or in business, my best outcomes have occurred when I had secondary choices that I liked almost as well as my primary one. Coming up with alternatives takes work, but for important transactions it is well worth the effort.

2. **Avoid going first.** This is tricky because sometimes you want to set the starting point for discussions. In negotiations, however, information is power, and knowing the opening terms that are acceptable to the

other side, before revealing your own, is generally preferable.

3. **Don't agree piecemeal.** The most significant transactions are often the most complex, and you don't want to agree to any single part of a transaction until all terms have been fully discussed. Good negotiators continually ask: *"Is there anything else you want?"* Only when the answer to that question is *"No"* do they begin seriously discussing terms, and then they agree to no single piece of the transaction without agreement on all issues.

4. **Know when to walk.** Always go into transactions knowing the worst price or terms you are willing to accept. If you know your bottom line *before* you enter into negotiations, you greatly reduce the risk of agreeing to a bad deal.

5. **Put time on your side.** Whenever possible, plan ahead so you are not forced by time, and/or financial constraints, into a bad deal. As importantly, don't allow your impatience, or the other party, to accelerate negotiations faster than your ability to analyze the transaction. *Assume nothing, and do not ever agree to anything you don't fully understand!*

Last, as a job-seeker or junior employee, it's a bad idea to negotiate too hard for the last dollar of compensation. At this early stage of your career, the important thing is to find the right opportunity and perform at a high level. If you do that, and if you're in the right position at the right organization, it's likely that you'll soon be given what you want. If you aren't, and you've proved yourself to be a valuable member of the team, *that's* when you become a tough negotiator—especially if you have other job opportunities in your back pocket.

WHY ME

When I speak to students, I'm often asked *"Why do you think you were chosen to be the Co-CEO of Greenwich Capital?"* And they're always surprised when I say, *"It's because of the Tumble Inn."*

Beer and Bonds

The Tumble Inn was a fun and lucrative side interest to my primary job of working at the bank. Even more importantly, this night job taught me a lesson about leadership that I brought back to my day job.

It may seem like quite a leap to take lessons learned from owning a bar and apply them to managing a major corporation, but it isn't. *All business owners and corporate CEOs, whether they're selling bonds, beer, or anything in between, have two primary goals every workday—they want to increase revenues and decrease expenses.* This had become second nature to me because, for the past seven years, I had been responsible for all business issues concerning the Tumble Inn. So, like everyone else at Greenwich Capital, I attended to my assigned duties, but I also approached my job as a bond salesman like an owner.

The best example of this came after I had been at the

firm for just over a year. The boss of our department, Gary Holloway, hired a trader from one of our major competitors. This trader had a good reputation, and everyone had high hopes that he would be a great addition to our department—but he wasn't.

After just a few days, it became clear that he would not put competitive prices on bond sales or purchases with clients. I, and others, spoke to him about this, but to no avail. Why he was so gun-shy, I don't know. But it didn't matter: he was rapidly squandering the valuable customer franchise we had worked so hard to build. However, nobody was anxious to tell Gary that his new hire was a bust.

Finally, despite being one of the most junior people in the department, I walked into Gary's office, explained the unvarnished truth about the new trader, and told Gary that he had to remove the new guy *"right now."* It was obvious that Gary was not happy to hear this news and, looking down at the papers on his desk, he said wearily, *"Okay Ben, I'll look into it."* Rather than taking the hint that it was time to leave, I waited three beats and said,

> *Gary, that's not good enough. You have to do this TODAY—if you wait any longer you might not have a business left to save.*

Gary's head snapped up, he looked me in the eyes and barked, *"I HEARD YOU THE FIRST TIME—NOW GET THE HELL OUT OF MY OFFICE!"* But despite his anger, Gary checked with the sales and trading managers, and the next day the new guy was gone. Gary treated me differently after that because he now knew that I would do whatever it took to ensure the firm was protected and successful.

It's worth noting that I not only identified a problem, but also proposed a solution. Just going into Gary's office and telling him the new trader was hurting our business would simply have dumped a problem in his lap. Telling Gary that the trader needed to be *"removed right now"* was important because, sadly, that was the correct solution. Herein lies the full lesson: *Think and act like an owner by identifying problems, coming up with solutions, and following them through to resolution.*

While the Tumble Inn and Greenwich Capital were for-profit enterprises, the fundamental principle of staying focused on the overall mission of your organization is equally important in the non-profit world.

Not the Smartest

While thinking like an owner set me apart from most other employees, another trait was equally significant.

After Ted, Rick Garth was the most important person at Greenwich Capital when I joined. But Rick had a much harder edge than Ted, which was probably a good thing because, as Head of Risk, Rick had a tough job: managing all the traders as well as his own trading account.

When Rick retired, he moved to Colorado to raise his family and became one of my clients. I always enjoyed talking to him because he was smart and I appreciated his rough humor, which, along with bonds, we traded back and forth.

One day, as our conversation touched on Greenwich Capital, I mentioned something positive about the firm.

Rather than ripping me with a wisecrack, Rick replied, *"You know, I think you should run Greenwich someday."* I mumbled, *"That would be nice,"* but he wouldn't let it go and added,

> *I'm serious, you're the most enthusiastic person at the firm about the firm and that's what it takes.*

While it was great to hear that vote of confidence, it's also important to note what Rick *didn't* say. He didn't say I was the smartest—only the most enthusiastic—but to Rick, that's what mattered most.

FOR YOU

Here are four questions for you to consider.

1. Can you think of someone you know who leads by example?

2. Can you think of a time when you led by example? Or failed to?

3. Do you come up with solutions to other people's problems? What are some examples? Could you apply your problem-solving ability at an internship or job?

4. What personal strengths can you draw on to be a leader?

Chapter 6

Exploring Careers

During the past year, I've spoken to over 100 groups of students, U.S. military personnel, and other organizations including the U.S. Ski Team. The question that concerns audiences the most is how to choose a career. This makes perfect sense to me because, ultimately, you must get this decision right if you want to realize your professional hopes and dreams.

PASSION AND TALENT

When it comes to choosing a career, the pronouncement you will typically hear is: *"Follow your passion and do what you love."* Despite how sensible and positive that sounds, I believe this advice is overly simplistic and sometimes dangerous.

If what you love to do is identical to what you have talent for, *or what you truly believe you can develop a talent for,* then there's no conflict. Go full speed ahead and pursue that job and career. However, if you're like many people and your passion is not aligned with your talents, I suggest you give serious consideration to doing what you *enjoy* for a hobby and utilizing your *talents* in your career.

How well you perform in competition directly affects how happy you are during the game, and this is multiplied *dramatically* when your professional opportunities and compensation are tied to your performance in the work world. This hit me on a gut level by having witnessed the agony my father endured from pursuing a job he was ill-suited for, and this same issue played out painfully early in my own career.

MY FAILURE

I had been at Greenwich Capital for only two years when the founder of the firm, Ted Knetzger, came by my desk and asked if I could have a hamburger with him after work. At dinner, Ted opened the conversation by complimenting my work as a salesman, and saying that he wanted to develop my skills further by making me a trader. When Ted suggested this, I was *SO* excited because I had always wanted to trade and was certain that I would be a *great* trader. On the spot, I accepted Ted's proposition.

As a salesman—at Bankers, Morgan Stanley, and Greenwich—my job had been to recommend ideas to clients, and the firm would make money buying and selling bonds with my clients' money. As a trader, my job was now to buy and sell bonds with Greenwich's money—a position that carried greater risk and reward for both the firm and myself.

The next day, with boundless enthusiasm, I began my new job and over the next two years proved myself to be one of *THE* all-time *WORST* traders in the history of Wall

Street. This doesn't mean I bankrupted the company: I was only a junior trader with junior trading limits. But I did display an uncanny ability to consistently lose money. At the end of those two miserable years, it was obvious that my career needed to turn in a different direction.

There was only one thing I was dead set against—going back to my old job in sales as *"a failure."* Around this time, Ted called me into his office. I felt uneasy as he closed the door and motioned for me to sit down. His opening comment was, *"Ben, having you trade is not working out."* No surprise there. But Ted did surprise me when he said, *"I want you to be the Chief Financial Officer."*

Actually, I wasn't surprised—I was shocked. I had assumed that my failure as a trader was an indelible stain on my resume, but CFO was one of the top five positions in the firm: *somehow I had failed upward!* Despite my excitement about this remarkable stroke of good fortune, and because it was so unexpected, I asked Ted for a few days to think about it.

Getting Lucky

Before I could get back to Ted, my world—and body—exploded. I had what's called an aortic dissection. This condition is rare, and it means that the main artery—which all your blood travels through—has a tear in it. People who experience this often die quickly from internal bleeding. It happened while I was at work; I felt fine and then suddenly the pain in my chest was excruciating. After I was taken to the local hospital's ER and Leigh arrived at my room, I whispered to her weakly,

I don't know what's going to happen, but I want you
to know how much I love you and the girls.

Leigh, realizing I was saying goodbye, immediately
stepped into the hallway and screamed, *"MY HUSBAND IS*
DYING AND NEEDS A DOCTOR—RIGHT NOW!" Afterwards,
my surgeon told me there was no doubt that Leigh saved
my life because I *was* dying and made it to surgery with
only minutes to spare.

While I never saw the *"white flash"* reported by some
people with near-death episodes, I did have one unforget-
table experience. After I left intensive care and thought I
was on the road back to "normal," my surgeon stopped by
and described a very different future:

You'll need many more major surgeries to repair
the damage to your aorta. (I've now had seven.) *And*
you can't run or lift anything heavy for the rest of
your life.

After he left, my spirits began crashing into a darkness I
didn't know existed—when suddenly I saw four words, in
white lettering, floating in the darkness: *"Everything Will*
Be Okay." Immediately the darkness disappeared and I felt
a surge of well-being and optimism beyond anything I had
ever experienced.

Soon after that, while still in the hospital, I called Ted
and told him, *"I don't want to be the CFO—I want to go back*
into sales." That's right—I was asking to return to my former
and much less prestigious job, which was also the one job in

the entire world that I, only weeks before, had said I didn't want! So, what changed?

What changed was that my near-death experience had stripped away my ego and left me wiser. I no longer cared about *"looking like a failure."* I only cared about doing a job I could perform at an elite level, that would help the company, and that was in sales.

A couple weeks later I went back to my old job with a renewed *appreciation* for doing something I was good at, and a renewed *determination* to make a major contribution to the firm. I accomplished that goal and rode that success to become the Sales Manager, Co-Chief Operating Officer, and finally Co-CEO.

Three Lessons from My Failure

1. **Professional success creates professional happiness.** While there are exceptions, I have personally experienced, and observed in others, this dynamic throughout my life and career. More often than not, it matters less what a person is doing than if they are able to do it well. Success generates interesting career opportunities, and the surest way to achieve success is to pursue a career that utilizes your talents.

   Since this advice differs markedly from the standard "follow your passion," I often get push back from students who ask, *"Are you telling me to get a job that uses my talents—even if that job will make me unhappy?"* My answer is that if you find a job you can do well, and you're respected by your co-workers, it's likely that you'll be very happy—even if what you're doing hasn't always been your passion. Conversely, if you pursue a career that follows your passion, but you don't have—or can't develop—the talent to be *professionally* successful at it, you're likely to be very unhappy.

Knowing in advance whether you can develop a certain talent is difficult, and internships may provide valuable insights. You may need to do a job, however, to find out how good you are at it.

2. **Continuing to be a good teammate** was my greatest success during my failure. It was a scary time because I saw my career beginning to mirror my father's. Even as I floundered, however, I kept encouraging and congratulating my co-workers, and doing everything I could think of to help them succeed. This convinced Ted and my co-workers that, despite being a terrible trader, I could still be a leader.

3. **You can't rely solely on your talent.** The big leagues are way too competitive for that. You also need a strong dose of determination—which I only fully acquired after my failure.

WHAT ARE YOUR TALENTS?

If you embrace my advice to do what you're good at, how do you decide what that is? For some people, this is an easy question to answer. My middle daughter, Kendall, has known her entire life that she wanted to be a doctor, and her strength, academically, is in the sciences. But for most of us, it isn't nearly so clear.

Four Ways to Help You Explore Careers

1. **Ask experienced professionals** who know you—parents, friends, friends' parents, professors, coaches, or career counselors—what they think your talents are, and what careers might be good fits for you. *Most people need guidance choosing their future because the work world is a complicated place with numerous paths you can take. The more people you ask for help, the better.*

2. **Take a personality and career test.** The purpose of these tests is to match your skills and interests to appropriate careers. "Meyers Briggs" and "Strong" are two of the best-known companies in this field. But don't put *too* much stock in their analysis: I recently took one of these tests and its #1 recommendation for me was to be a *Parks and Recreation Manager*—which is a good job, but it wouldn't have been right for me. These tests, however, are likely to suggest some career paths you should consider.

3. **Trial and Error.** Try internships in the field you might want to work in. For future searches, you will have hard-earned experience about what you liked and didn't like about past industries, organizations, and jobs. Statistically, you will have 8–10 different jobs in your career and, over time, you should get better and better at choosing a career.

4. **Look in the mirror.** No matter how much input you receive, *you must own this issue.* It's your life and

you will live with the career consequences—often for
40 years. So seek lots of advice, consider it all care-
fully, but remember that no one knows you better
than you.

GO WITH GROWTH

The perfect situation is to be in a rapidly *growing* industry,
at an organization that's successful and *growing,* in a
capacity that's *growing* in importance. That's a lot to ask
for, but understanding the importance of growth will help
you compare various opportunities and focus on the fields,
organizations, and jobs that offer the most potential.

The old expression, *"A rising tide lifts all boats"* applies
here, and my career is a good example. During my first 25
years on Wall Street, the markets were in a historic boom.
My principal employer, Greenwich Capital, grew quickly,
and salespeople were central to our firm's success. Clearly,
the tide was rising. However, the waters receded abruptly
during the credit crisis of 2008, and most financial companies, including Greenwich, contracted.

The obvious question is, *"Where can I get tide charts
for the economy?"* Unfortunately, they don't exist. But
what you *can* do is understand that some industries and
jobs are inherently more volatile than others, and talk with
many professionals in your field to get a sense of an organization's potential to grow.

Finally, it's healthy to appreciate that professional
success is not entirely within your control. Many professionals will admit that luck played a significant role in their
careers—count me in that group. Understanding this will

keep you from feeling too much like a hero when things go well, or too much like a bum when they go poorly.

LARGE OR SMALL

The question is, "Would you rather begin your career at a large or small organization?" All things being equal, I'd vote for a large organization because they often have:

- **Training programs** that are structured to quickly educate you on the business generally and your job specifically.

- **Multiple products and/or services** that can give you a broad exposure to the industry.

- **Many employees** who will be your training-program classmates and co-workers. Over time, the majority of these folks will move on to other organizations in the industry. These contacts can later prove invaluable when you're looking for new job opportunities, searching to hire strong performers as managers, or selling products.

An additional benefit is that future employers, probably correctly, will assume that getting a job at a large and respected organization was highly competitive and you made the cut. Also, they will likely believe that you have been well-trained. My advice about starting at a large organization does, however, have some caveats:

- **Businesses with fewer than 500 workers** employ more than half of the U.S. workforce, so there's a good chance that a small business may offer you the best opportunity.

- **Large organizations are concentrated in urban centers**, and if that's not where you want to live, the likelihood of working for a large organization diminishes.

- **Joining a small organization with good growth prospects**, and working for a boss who will look out for your best interests, can be superior to signing on with any large organization.

WHY MY CAREER WORKED FOR ME

I didn't end up working in finance because it was a passion of mine or because I studied it in school. Bowdoin College didn't offer any courses in finance, and I knew next to nothing about the industry. I was a Government major and, while no great student, I did enjoy my law-related courses, so becoming a lawyer seemed logical. However, since I was clueless about how corporations operated, I decided I should work for a few years before law school. Bowdoin's Career Services office recommended I look into banking because of its broad exposure to many different businesses.

A question students often ask me is, *"Did you love the finance industry?"* The answer is, *"No, but I did love my career."* The distinction is that while I found finance and the markets interesting, they never became a passion. What I *was* passionate about was working in a fast-paced and competitive environment, being a contributor on a winning team, and supporting my family.

YOUR CHOOSE-A-CAREER STEW

The recipe for your Choose-A-Career Stew includes the following four steps.

STEP 1: List your personality traits that an employer might find attractive. Examples are being: *energetic, strategic, empathetic, hard-working, self-starting, competitive, organized, analytical, dependable, adaptable, confident, determined, resilient, outgoing, eager to learn, as well as being a good communicator/ listener/teammate/leader.*

STEP 2: List your skills that an employer might find attractive. Examples of such skills include: *music, math, foreign languages, computer programming, information technology, writing, public speaking, researching, administration, athletics, acting, creativity, teaching, negotiating,* and *sales.*

STEP 3: List the lifestyle issues that are important to you. Examples include: *compensation, location, hours, helping others, social causes, personal growth, pace or variety of work, physical and social work environment.*

STEP 4: Combine the following:

- Your personality/skills/lifestyle lists.
- Advice from this chapter of *The Bigs.*
- Insights or ideas gained from your personality and career tests.
- Suggestions from professionals about careers that play to your strengths.

From this kettle of information, you can then choose careers that most interest you. In the future, you will also add your professional experiences to the pot.

Few people choose the best career for themselves on their first attempt. I thought I wanted to be a lawyer, then a banker, then a trader, before realizing that sales and management were where I belonged. *The important thing is for you to learn the process of how to choose a career— so with each new position you take, you will be getting closer to finding the best field, organization, and position to pursue your hopes and dreams.*

YOUR MOST VALUABLE ASSET

It's a mistaken but widely accepted notion that students have lots of time to figure out what to do with their lives. The fact is, your time is precious and you have much to do: explore career paths, get the necessary education and training to walk those paths, and begin your professional journey. The sooner you begin, the greater your chances of success.

As each year goes by, time becomes even more precious—*especially* if you want to have a family. I changed jobs or companies four times within six years after graduation. But the stress of those changes was modest because I didn't yet have any children to support. When I failed as a trader, the stakes were much higher because Avery was four, Kendall was a newborn, and Leigh had stopped working. But while I was in the *wrong job*, I had found the *right company.*

If you plan on having a family, statistics tell us you have

only 8–10 years from when you receive your college degree to when your first child arrives. Use those valuable years to take risks and try to find the right position in a company that's right for you.

HOLD OUT OR SIGN ON

When I'm speaking to students, a question I regularly get is, *"Should I hold out for the job I really want, or settle for something less?"* While there is no one-size-fits-all answer to this issue, I do have some advice.

Especially for your first job, you should be more concerned about *where* you work than whether the position is perfect or prestigious. If you get a job with an organization you're excited about, and then do a great job, better opportunities within that organization are likely to arise reasonably quickly. If they don't, you now have experience in your field and will be a more compelling candidate for the position you want at other organizations.

ADVICE FOR SPECIFIC INDUSTRIES

As mentioned earlier, virtually all the advice in *The Bigs* applies to all industries. This section, however, addresses specific issues that are relevant to some fields that are popular with students.

Socially-Focused Careers

For many people the desire to help others is more important than wealth. In most cases, people who work in non-profit organizations, education, or social work make less money than their peers in for-profits companies. This is a sacrifice that is made by these professionals, and one that should be recognized and appreciated. The question is: Are these professionals also sacrificing happiness?

A Gallup survey of 450,000 Americans, across all professions and income levels, suggests the answer is no. The survey revealed that respondents' happiness initially increased with more money, but their happiness stopped rising at an annual income of $75,000—a level of compensation ultimately attainable in most for-profit and not-for-profit organizations. Additionally, this survey examined only the relationship between people's income and their happiness. It did not evaluate the job satisfaction of helping others— which for most socially-focused professionals is a huge benefit to their work.

Because the choice between focusing on income or social issues is so personal, many people have strong opinions on this topic. *Listen to all the advice you receive, but base your decision on just ONE factor—what will make YOU the happiest.*

Highly Technical Careers

Highly technical careers come in many different flavors. Popular ones include medicine, law, engineering, technology, and science—though numerous other fields also require specialized knowledge and training.

Many students make the mistake of believing that professionals in highly technical positions don't need the kinds of information and advice in *The Bigs*. These students think that, for them, the real world will be like school—all they need to do is study hard and their knowledge will carry them forward to successful careers.

My daughter Kendall was a perfect example of this mindset. When she was a pre-med sophomore at Bowdoin College, I asked her to read an early draft of *The Bigs* and she gave me some very helpful feedback. But as a senior, Kendall explained to me her new situation:

> *When I first read The Bigs I liked it because you wrote it and I thought the stories were fun. But I didn't think that most of the information and advice applied to me because I wanted to be a doctor. Now that I'm applying for internships before medical school, I'm using ALL the information and advice about networking and interviewing.*

It doesn't matter how smart you are, or how valuable your skills are. Following the advice in *The Bigs* about how to choose, get, and do a great job will significantly enhance your chances of achieving your hopes and dreams.

Long-Shot Careers

Unless you are ridiculously talented, a host of careers and career goals are a long shot. Examples include becoming a rock star, a celebrity actor/actress, or a professional athlete.

If your dream career falls into the category of a long shot, what should you do? Unfortunately, as with the tide charts, there is no clear answer. But when students tell me they want to pursue a long-shot career, I encourage them to do two things:

1. **Research the likelihood of being successful** in their career goals. This information may well *not* influence their decision, but anytime you embark on a new project, do so with your eyes open.

2. **Consider whether there is a related career path** that would align with their talents and interests and be less of a long shot.

If a student understands the odds of success and is determined to pursue a long-shot career, I tell them, *"That's great—congratulations!"* Why? Because they will need this kind of informed determination. But they also need one more thing—a plan.

Specifically, this plan should have a time frame for reevaluating their career choice. For instance, after you finish your education, if you want to move to Hollywood and become an actor/actress, or are an athlete who enters professional sports, you should plan how long to pursue this career if you don't make significant progress. How much time you should give your long shot is up to you. But what you *can't* do is wait tables or park cars for so long that it's impossible to redirect your career.

This advice directly ties into our discussion of passion and happiness—because it will be very difficult for you to be happy following your long-shot passion if it doesn't lead to professional success. Also, as a student, you can't allow your dreams of long-shot success to distract you from preparing for other opportunities.

Most importantly, if you're going for a long shot, give it your *BEST* shot. While this may not lead to the success you hoped for, the pursuit of a long shot will give you practiced determination and focus for your next career.

FOR YOU

Here are two questions for you to consider.

1. What careers would you like to explore, and why do those careers appeal to you? How will you go about exploring those careers?

2. How do you feel about *The Bigs'* advice that the surest path to professional success is to do what you're good at?

Chapter 7

Staying Out
of Big Trouble

Every single day you're in danger of getting into big trouble. The forms it takes are infinite, and the risks to your career, happiness, and even your life are real.

THREE STORIES

Here are three very different stories—personal, professional, and financial—concerning big trouble. Regardless of how talented you are, or successful you become, if you don't avoid big trouble, none of that will matter.

Telephone Pole

When I think about the worst story from my teenage years, it still makes me shudder. I was the first in our group to get a license, so on our evenings out I was usually behind the wheel.

It was a hot summer night, the family wagon was packed with my buddies, the windows were down, and we

93

were all in high spirits. The wooded back road was like a roller coaster, and as we careened down the steepest hill, I decided it would be funny to turn off the headlights. I knew there was a slight left bend at the bottom of the hill, but now I couldn't see. It all happened so fast—I began to turn too late. Suddenly, I heard, and actually *felt,* a telephone pole *"WHOOSH"* by the right side of the wagon—I couldn't have missed it by more than an inch.

Six months later, during hockey season, we were playing our rivals from neighboring Pittsfield. As we skated warm-ups, I remember watching their best player. A few months earlier, he had been the driver on a night out with his friends. He crashed and one boy died and two were seriously injured. With a teenage self-centric viewpoint, but also correctly, I remember staring at him, shaking my head and thinking, *"His life will never be the same again, and that could have been me."*

Front Page News

Big trouble is not limited to your youth or your personal life. When I first started at Greenwich Capital, Gary Holloway told all new hires:

> *Don't ever do anything you don't want to see on the front page of the* New York Times *or* Wall Street Journal.

This is extraordinarily good advice, and the trouble that one of my customers got into illustrates what Gary was talking about.

I called him Hoops because he had been a high school basketball star in New Jersey. A few years older than me and already a successful trader for a large commodity firm, he became my client at Morgan Stanley and then Greenwich. Hoops was also lots of fun and he went out of his way to help educate me about the intricacies of the bond market.

But Hoops got into big trouble. With a salesman from another Wall Street firm, he agreed to do additional business in return for a kickback of a portion of the commissions his trades generated. When this arrangement came to light, the ramifications for Hoops were horrific. He was convicted of a crime and spent two years in jail; his wife left him; he was penniless from fines and legal fees; and when he got out of jail he was barred by the SEC from doing the one thing he was great at—trading.

For a while, Hoops was a one-man liquor wholesaler and I filled my basement with cases of his wine. But that, and other ventures, failed. The last I heard he had moved out West and was still struggling to piece his life back together.

Exactly Zero

Just as my career at Greenwich Capital was taking off, I learned an important lesson about money. It was February 2000, and I had been the Co-Chief Operating Officer for the past two years. Because the firm had done well, and I was now part of the management team, my income had increased. Aside from my ongoing health issues, I was feeling pretty good and had started accumulating some savings.

However, there was one problem: Many people I knew were investing in start-up technology companies whose stock prices were leaping into the stratosphere. Fortunes were being made overnight. After years of resisting the siren call of dot-com investments, some combination of envy and greed drove me to abandon my sensible investing plan and join the party. I sank 20% of my 1999 income into a video streaming start-up—which tech-savvy experts told me would *"quickly"* increase in value ten-fold.

Well, something did happen quickly. Before the ink was dry on my check, the dot-com boom imploded. Four months later, this fabulous *start-up* had *gone down,* and my entire investment was now worth exactly zero.

Money issues are rampant and can negatively affect most people's lives repeatedly, sometimes severely. Here are the three best ways to avoid big trouble with money:

1. **Control expenses:** Most people agree that money can't buy happiness, but that doesn't stop them from trying. Surveys have shown that Americans, at virtu-ally *every* income level, feel that they need twice as much money as they have to consider themselves financially secure. How can that be? It's simple— everyone spends too much. Even if your income is modest, if you control your spending, you will be part of a small minority that does not dread thinking about their finances.

2. **Have no discretionary debt:** There will likely be times during your life when you need to borrow money: financing college, or purchasing a home, fall into this

category. Happily, in most circumstances, the interest rate you'll pay on this type of debt is reasonably low.

However, you should only use *credit cards* for purchases you can afford to pay off *that month* because the interest rate charged on most cards is insanely high (sometimes *5 times* the rate charged on student loans or home mortgages).

This is a mistake that many students make. Don't be the sucker that all credit card companies want you to be—*master your MasterCard!*

3. **Know what you don't know:** This is a hugely important lesson that I, and most professionals, learned the hard way. One reason is that large portions of the financial services industry are built to convince people they can "beat the market." Over the long run, though, very few do. So, when you have savings to invest, what should you do? My mantra is to *"keep it simple and only invest in what you can understand."*

Specifically, I believe that most of your assets should be in diversified mutual funds—which are solid long-term investments. I also believe in the traditional asset allocation methodology of putting 100% minus your age into equity/stock funds (generally higher risk and higher reward), and the rest into fixed income or cash (generally lower risk and lower reward). If you don't understand this paragraph, don't worry. When you have money to invest, use my advice as the starting point for a discussion with whomever you choose as a financial advisor.

Finally, if you feel compelled to invest in an individual company (especially a small one or a start-up), or lend money to anyone, *never* part with more cash than you can afford to lose. Understand that there's a very real chance you could end up getting back *exactly zero.*

THE LESSON OF BIG TROUBLE

Success is earned by working hard and intelligently day after day for years and decades. But the lesson is that you can create life-altering trouble for yourself as quickly as a passing thought.

FOR YOU

Here are four questions for you to consider:

1. Have you thought about what impact your reckless acts can have on others?

2. What do you think about the trouble Hoops got into?

3. Do you feel ready to manage your finances? Do you have a credit card? Has it been a blessing or curse?

4. Whom can you go to for financial advice? Have you already received financial advice from that person(s)? What was that advice, and was it helpful?

Chapter 8

Happiness & Professional Success

My advice concerning happiness and professional success does *not* include waking up in the morning, singing Zippity-Do-Dah, grinning ear-to-ear, and sallying forth into the world thinking you're happy. That's not happiness—that's delusion. There is, however, one specific thing you can do that will *greatly* increase your average level of happiness.

HAPPINESS IS A CHOICE

One spring evening in 1996, I was hosting Greenwich Capital's annual post-golf-outing dinner. As was our custom, we hired a well-known guest speaker for the evening, and that year it was the famous basketball coach, Rick Pitino. It was an energetic room, packed with over 300 clients and employees.

A few months earlier, Coach Pitino had won the NCAA Championship with Kentucky and had recently been hired by the Boston Celtics. Rick had just received some bad

99

news, however. Due to the NBA's lottery system, the Celtics' two top draft picks (which could have been #1 and #2) would be #6 and #7—an unmitigated disaster. Coach Pitino told us what happened the next day:

> *A reporter called and asked me if I was upset by the bad luck of getting the two worst possible lottery picks. I told him the truth that yes, I had been very upset, but then I told him something else which was also true. Five minutes after I heard the news, I realized nobody was forcing me to be upset, and I made the conscious decision to choose not to be. Instead, I decided to channel my energy into making the draft picks I DID HAVE better than the draft picks I DIDN'T HAVE. Immediately, I was no longer upset. I was now focused and determined.*

These words were an epiphany. That evening, I resolved to *drastically* shorten the time I would allow myself to be annoyed or angry. Since I now understand that, in most circumstances, happiness is a choice, I know what to do:

- **If I *can* control what's making me unhappy**, I immediately start making plans to fix it. By doing that, I'm no longer focused on being angry—I'm focused on solving the problem.

- **If I *can't* control what's making me unhappy**, because it's already happened or it's beyond my powers to influence, I immediately hit what I call my *Emotional Reset Button* and try to accept whatever has occurred.

What used to take me hours, days, or weeks to get over, now generally takes me less than a minute. Also, if you're mad at someone in particular, why let that person continue to hurt you? Take control by moving on.

An example of a situation I "controlled" was my 22 bullet points to Avery. When I read her email asking if it was okay to start her new job a week late, I freaked out. That feeling quickly gave way, though, as I began composing and writing my advice to her. Suddenly, I was in a positive and problem-solving state of mind.

An example of a situation I could not control was my *"Everything Will Be Okay"* experience in the hospital. Interestingly, my health crisis occurred five years *before* my dinner with Coach Pitino, but my response was right out of his playbook. The aortic dissection had already occurred, my bleak prognosis was what it was, and the best course of action for my mental health, career, and family was to accept it—*right then*—and move forward.

While these two examples were of great significance to me, don't wait for such occasions to choose happiness. *The power of this principle lies in its becoming second nature.* Daily, we all encounter situations that upset or anger us: poor service at a restaurant, traffic jams, or a lost wallet. When something negative occurs, as often as possible, say to yourself, *"I can fix this by doing . . . "* or, *"This can't be fixed so I accept it."* If you start doing that NOW, the impact over your lifetime will be transformative.

THE GREATEST GIFT

When I speak to groups of college students about happiness, I can tell that some of them are thinking,

> *I'm happy enough, and the only reason I'm here is because I want to learn how to become a successful professional.*

But what they don't understand is that increasing their happiness will also significantly increase their chances for professional success. Why? Because *happiness is like a magnet—people want to work with, and for, happy people. And unhappiness is like a repellant—people don't want to work with, or for, unhappy people.*

Strive to appreciate how critical your happiness is to issues more important than your career. *Your mental and physical health will reflect your happiness, and THAT is the greatest gift you can give to the people who love you.*

FOR YOU

Here are two questions for you to consider:

1. Could you increase your happiness by shortening the amount of time you allow yourself to be unhappy?

2. What impact would that have on your life, your family, and friends?

Chapter 9

Next Steps

Following the 15 STEPS below will dramatically increase the likelihood of a fun and successful journey from college, to the real world, to achieving your hopes and dreams. Still, this is *not* a path to be followed blindly. You'll accomplish, ignore, customize, and add STEPS as you go along—and that's how it should be. Your life in the big leagues has the potential to be as compelling as any other adventure you can imagine. But having a plan that will continuously evolve is vital. So start with this one and then make it your own.

STEP 1: Choose to be happy by consciously shortening the amount of time you allow yourself to be upset. If you start today and do it as often as possible, it *will* transform your life—both personally and professionally. This single act will do more than any other to pave the way for you to achieve professional success. (*Pgs 99–102*)

STEP 2: Write a short essay about what career(s) interest you most. Writing will force you to organize your thoughts on this critical issue. If you haven't yet chosen a career, follow the four-step recipe to create your Choose-a-Career Stew. Choosing a career is the first step in your preparation for the big leagues. You can always change course in the future, but to begin exploring and learning about the work world, it is helpful to focus on a specific career(s) now. (*Pgs 81–91*)

STEP 3: Look for organizations and clubs to join that relate to your professional interests. These groups can be from inside or outside of school.

STEP 4: Read news and watch shows that relate to your interests. For example, if you're interested in fashion, farming, finance, marketing, medicine, law, government, teaching, global health, the environment, or virtually any major industry or issue, there are regularly published articles about organizations in these fields in *The New York Times* and *The Wall Street Journal.*

You should subscribe to one of these papers online and read it daily. The NYT has a special digital copy rate for students, currently $1 per week, a remarkable bargain for the information and entertainment you will receive. Here are other examples of how media can help you get up to speed: if you're interested in the stock and bond markets, watch CNBC; if you want to start a business, watch *Shark Tank;* to pursue fashion, watch the Fashion TV channel.

STEP 5: Have your resume ready. If you don't have one, it's likely that Career Services will help you write one. If that's not the case, search "resume writing tips." Do this *now* because internship and job opportunities can arise anytime. When asked for your resume, you want to be able to say, *"I'll send it right now."*

STEP 6: Have your uniform ready. While you don't need formal "interview clothes" to have on-campus informational interviews with fellow students, you never know when an internship/job opportunity might come along. When one does, you want to be able to say, *"I'd love to get together, I'm available whenever's convenient for you."* If you don't have interview clothes appropriate for your career interests, it's time to go shopping. (*Pgs 40–41*)

STEP 7: Visit your college's Career Services office during September of *each* school year—starting freshman year. Meet with a professional there and explain that you would like help in getting a summer internship. You need to do this early in the fall because many of the best internships go quickly. Remember, the earlier you ask ALL your contacts about internship opportunities, the more likely you are to land one. Also, try to develop an ongoing and positive relationship with the staff at Career Services.

Think of your interactions with the career counselors as an interview—you want these professionals on your side because they often have close relationships with employers. To obtain great internships and jobs, sometimes these Career Services professionals can be as important to you as having a strong academic record. (*Pgs 11, 27–28*)

STEP 8: Strive to have your part-time job relate to your field of interest. Almost 80% of students work an average of 19 hours per week during the school year. If you're in this group, you should try to get a job that relates to your career interests. If restaurants or hotels interest you, try to get a job there; teaching or coaching, try local schools and teams; a specific business, knock on the door and explain why you'd like to work there. Another approach is to get a job that allows you to study while working (such as a library monitor or a night-time babysitter). You may well be forced to settle for a position simply for the cash, but you should first exhaust all avenues to find employment that furthers either your academic or professional career ambitions.

This advice about seeking positions that double as internships also applies to summer jobs. (*Pgs 10–11*)

STEP 9: Start building your contact list now. Set an initial goal of at least 20 prospects—with a minimum of three coming from your college's Career Services alumni data base, and a few being seniors at your college who will soon be working in your field. Before your first job search is in full bloom, your contact list should contain well over 100 names and continue to grow throughout your career. (*Pgs 16–19*)

STEP 10: Begin your informational interviews freshman year of college. If you're attending a four-year college, complete at least two as a freshman, and try to double that number each year (2, 4, 8, 16). Start with the seniors at your school who are going into your industry. Write a short report after each interview, highlighting what you learned and what you need to follow up on. Remember to send thank-you notes after *all* informational interviews. (*Pgs 19–26*)

STEP 11: Try to get an internship after your freshman and/or sophomore year of college. These internships will prepare you to compete strongly for junior-year internships that can lead to job offers. Freshmen/ sophomore internships are scarce and are often given by family, friends, or alumni to whoever asks first. You want to be that first student to apply—which means contacting professionals and organizations in your network about internships no later than September of each year. (*Pgs 10–15*)

STEP 12: Identify internship and job opportunities. Employment websites are useful, but most of the best opportunities are likely to emerge from your networking efforts and informational interviews. You must be creative, aggressive, and persistent in uncovering internship/job openings. Also, fully utilize the resources of your college's Career Services office for this critical task. (*Pgs 27–28*)

STEP 13: Bring your A game to all internship and job interviews. To hook and land a great job, you need to be confident that you're the best person for the position, and then tell the interviewer why. This confidence comes from matching your talents with a job and having dozens of informational interviews with professionals in that field. You also need to prepare for these interviews by practicing the five most commonly asked interview questions. Finally, remember to always "close strong."(*Pgs 28–41*)

STEP 14: After you get a great job, send thank-you notes to *everyone* who helped you in *any* way. It's not only the right thing to do, but it's also likely you will need help again from these people during your career. (*Pgs 42–44*)

STEP 15: Maximize your great internship or job opportunity. Remember my first bullet point to Avery: *"Don't strive to do a good job; strive to do an outstanding job."* Also, strive to be a leader your very first day on the job, and always think like an owner. (*Pgs 59–63*)

If you have questions, you can send me an email by going to www.thebigsproject.com and clicking on the "CONTACT" tab.

Letter

The Biggest Step

Since publication of the original *Bigs* two years ago, a question that college students often ask me is, *"What's the most important thing I need to do to be successful?"* My answer is that the *biggest* step to achieving your life goals is to *BE EXCITED.*

Why is this so important? It's because excitement is contagious, and every organization knows that its *best* employees and leaders are excited about what they do. For highly sought-after positions, you will need to show excitement about *doing* the job in order to make an interviewer excited about hiring you *for* the job. This applies to summer jobs, internships, and every position you aspire to throughout your career.

Reading *The Bigs* has provided you a solid understanding about what works—and what doesn't work—in the real world, and you now have a significant head start on your peers. If you keep *The Bigs* at hand and refer to it as challenges arise, you will both lengthen that lead and give yourself a great chance of achieving your professional hopes and dreams.

I'm rooting for you!

Your Friend,

Ben

A special thanks to Geoff Marchant, my high-school English teacher and friend, and his wife Kathy, for their skillful editing of The Bigs.

The Bigs Career Exploration Program

MISSION

To provide high school and college students the career skills needed to achieve their hopes and dreams.

OVERVIEW

There are two Bigs Career Exploration Programs—one for high schools and one for colleges—each with a video and textbook that are tailored to speak directly and clearly to that group.

> **Colleges** have shown the most interest in doing the program for their freshmen so they can benefit from the information throughout their college careers.

> **High schools** are looking for meaningful and engaging programs for their second-semester seniors; therefore, many schools choose to do The Bigs Program for their seniors during the winter or spring.

The Bigs Career Exploration Program:

- **Helps individual students** become productive and happy professionals. This is the primary goal of *The Bigs*. Specifically, career exploration helps students be thoughtful about which courses to study and what organizations to join; how to get internships and jobs; and how to do a great job and be a leader.

- **Promotes equal opportunity** for students without a deep reservoir of family-centered professional advice and contacts.

- **Enhances the reputation of high schools and colleges with their students, parents, and alumni.** For independent schools, this will generate increased monetary support and a stronger applicant pool. For public schools, this will lead to increased support from all stakeholders.

- **Teaches students career skills** that will allow them to be more productive employees and entrepreneurs—leading to higher employment.

Two additional benefits of The Bigs Program apply only to high schools:

- **An experiential learning program for high schools** that want their seniors to put *The Bigs* information and advice to use outside the classroom. For schools that already offer experiential learning, The Bigs Program provides seniors the tools to maximize that experience.

- **A blueprint for *all* high school students.** One-third, or more than one million, high school graduates don't attend college. For these students it's even more important to receive career training in high school because they need to know *right now* how to choose, get, and do a great job.

THE BIGS PROGRAM

This program has three components:

1. **A Bigs Video.** This video contains six modules, each 5 minutes long. Questions after each module help facilitate a discussion among students and the school's education professionals and/or alumni. The six modules are:
   - **Hopes and Dreams**
   - **Starting a Business**
   - **Exploring Careers**
   - **Getting Internships and Jobs**
   - **Doing a Great Job and Being a Leader**
   - **Next Steps**

2. **Each student is given a copy of *The Bigs*** and encouraged to use it as a resource throughout their academic and professional careers.

3. **Parents can be notified that their student has been given a copy of *The Bigs,*** and schools often encourage parents to read the book and discuss these career issues with their children.

SCHEDULING THE BIGS PROGRAM

This program is designed to give schools flexibility in scheduling—both in the size and number of Bigs Sessions. For example, schools can provide The Bigs Program in:

- **One session** by showing the 30-minute Bigs Video to a group in an auditorium, conducting a panel discussion, and handing out copies of *The Bigs* to all students.

- **Six sessions** by showing one of the 5-minute video modules and spending the rest of the session discussing that specific issue. This can be done in large or small groups, and copies of *The Bigs* would be given to students during the first session.

CONTACTING THE BIGS PROGRAM

Interested educational professionals, parents, alumni, and students can contact Ben Carpenter at ben@thebigs project.com, or Lynn Siegel, Head of Bigs Outreach, at lynn@thebigsproject.com. We will be happy to arrange a call to see how The Bigs Program can help your students and school.

Appendix

Family and Friends

In the big leagues, no one does it on their own. *The Bigs* explained how to use your network to achieve *your* hopes and dreams, but this is a two-way street. As you progress in your job search and career, there will be many chances to share what you've learned. Seize these moments! There are two other condensed versions of *The Bigs:*

- **For High School Students**

- **For Transitioning U.S. Military Personnel**

If you have family or friends in these stages of life, why not tell them about *The Bigs?* Working to realize hopes and dreams is not easy for anyone. However, sharing the lessons from *The Bigs* will greatly increase the likelihood of success for the people you care about most.

If you have a younger brother, sister, friend, or cousin in high school, they need this version of *The Bigs.* This book will inspire them to dream—and give them the tools to take action.

Available on Amazon in Print and Kindle

In partnership with the USO, this *Bigs* book is being written to help U.S. military personnel with their transition back into the civilian workforce. It is gratifying to help those who have sacrificed so much to protect all of us.

Available Soon on Amazon in Print and Kindle

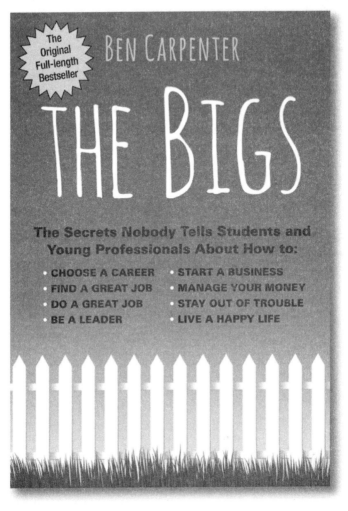

If you enjoyed the condensed *Bigs,* and want to gain an even *BIGGER* edge for your professional career, then the original Amazon five-star bestseller, with three times more stories and how-to-get-it-done advice, is for you. This book was written for my daughter Avery, but the stories and lessons apply to *everyone* who's looking to enter, or re-enter, the workforce.

Available on Amazon in Print, Kindle, and Audio Editions